Brandon-
  Thank you
to so many i
watching your videos had made
me laugh uncontrollably!
Thank you for that! I've
enclosed many items from our
walk of life - most are for Bo's
Heavenly clubhouse; our charity
since the death of our sweet
son. Keep being the light to so
many in such tough times

  with so much love,
  Amanda Hartwig

From Heaven.

Through Hell.

To Heaven.

The Story Behind Bo's Heavenly Clubhouse

Amanda Hartwig

This book is dedicated to the sweetest, happiest little boy.

Your story may have been brief, but it is one that will enlighten and inspire many people for years to come.

Thank you for making your mark on the world, little one. Thank you for making your mark on me, Bo William Hartwig.

Though you are gone from our sight, you will never be forgotten. We look forward to the day that we can hold you again. We remember that another day without you is another day closer to seeing you. My wish is to pass on your legacy. I hope to let everyone know that you were here, and that you made a difference. You're still making a difference today. You've impacted so many people, Bo, and you still are. I will continue to say your name for the rest of my life. We refuse to stay silent. We love you so much!

To Infinity and Beyond.

Psalm 34:18 – The Lord is close to the brokenhearted and saves those who are crushed in spirit.

FOREWORD

"Bo's Heavenly Clubhouse has given me life after death on Earth. The sheer amount of support and love that Bo's spreads to parents of child loss, like myself, is immeasurable. It's a family founded on circumstances no one wants to find themselves in, but cannot get through alone. I will forever be grateful to have Bo's as not only a resource, but a family of others like me."

Veronica Gerhardstein
In Loving Memory of her beloved son, Avery

"Then they cried to the Lord in their trouble, and He saved them from their distress. He sent out His Word and healed them; He rescued them from the grave." Psalm 107:19-20

"Amanda is an exceptional person who makes selfless contributions to her community, friends and child loss families. I have been blessed to have her in my life as a friend and fellow child loss mom. I am thankful for Bo's Heavenly Clubhouse, where I have had the opportunity to meet other grieving parents. It is within those meetings that I have experienced the most pivotal part in my grieving and healing process. Amanda, please continue making a difference, I appreciate all that you have done for me and my family!"

Heidi Soba
"You can't give up, it's impossible."
In Loving Memory of her beloved daughter, Alexis Soba

"Despite the hardship of losing an infant child, Amanda continues to provide love, empathy, and friendship to all who she comes in contact with. With strength that she has developed from this loss, Amanda created Bo's Heavenly Clubhouse; A support for bereaved parents. Through all of this, Amanda strives to be the best God-fearing woman, mother, wife, friend, and leader in all that she does."

Sue Mitchell Metz
"Suicide has no hold on us, who are left to finish your story."
In Loving Memory of her beloved son, Ryan Mitchell.

"I can do all things through Christ who strengthens me."
Philippians 4:13

"Amanda has been one of the greatest people in my life since the death of my son, Maxwell. She reminds me that there is always a reason to keep going and a way to find happiness after anything. I've never met someone so dedicated to helping others."

Erin Marie Bennett
"A person's a person, no matter how small!"- Dr. Seuss
In Loving Memory of her beloved son, Maxwell Thelonious Bennett.

Imagine for A Moment

Visiting your child's grave.
Your baby.
The one that you spent 12 hours
In labor with.
The one that you gave birth to.
The little whimpered cry when they were born.
The one that you spent hours with,
Awake and sleep deprived at night.
The one who would smile,
At everything, all the time.
The one that you held ever so tightly.
Snuggled in and close to your heart.
The boo-boo's that you kissed,
The mischief that was made.
The goofy laughs together.
The blissfulness of innocence.
Just imagine.
Gone.
Life as you know it,
Changing in a single instant.
Your world upside down.
Painted black and dreary.
Blanketed with shock.
Debilitated with excruciating pain.
Imagine.

Finding your precious baby.
Your sweet child not breathing.
And having to perform CPR.
Knowing in your heart that it's too late,
But praying to God,
That a miracle can happen.
Imagine.
Seeing the doctor shake her head.
Watching your baby's heart beat by a machine.
Covering them with tears.
And unending prayers.
Your beloved child died.
Imagine.
Clinging to old photographs.
Holding their favorite blanket or teddy bear,
That they once held onto.
Searching franticly for memories,
Anywhere.
Smelling their old clothes.
Watching your world fall apart.
Convincing yourself that you're not crazy.
That there really isn't,
"Anything you could have done!"
That we truly did all we could.
Your "normal" brain function,
Turned into shambles.
To relinquish all the control,
That you once thought that you possessed.
Imagine.
Rewinding time in your mind.
Constantly.

Living in the past.
Wishing so badly to go back.
Replaying memories.
Thinking, "If I only knew then."
"I could have done this" or "I should have."
Imagine.
The revolving hormones of pregnancy.
Mixed with the agony of child loss.
The excruciating pain of crying.
Until you couldn't breathe another moment.
Imagine.
Explaining to your other children,
Who their sibling is.
And why this tragedy happened.
Even though you promised,
That nothing bad would ever happen to them.
Imagine.
The next time you're up late at night.
And your baby is crying.
Or you're stressing out about a temper tantrum.
When you're ready to complain about parenting.
Stop.
Imagine.
That your precious child,
God forbid, not be here.
Not be here to hold or kiss.
To miss all the firsts with your child.
To not be able to see their milestones.
Imagine.
Having THIS be your reality.
Having to visit your beloved child at a cemetery.

With a headstone.
That reads your baby's name.
And your other children,
Seeing their sibling like this.
Imagine.
Just imagine.
Cherish.
Live.
Love.
Breaking the silence of child loss.

Introduction

Welcome to the club that nobody wants to be in, the boat that no one wants to be aboard, and the lonely days that no one wants to live through. But here we are. Yes, here we are. We have no choice but to be a member of this club, to never come ashore from this boat again. For as long as we live, we will forever be stripped of our innocence. We are the "strong ones." We are on a journey we never thought that we would be taking, but we are forced to walk because of a tremendous amount of devastatingly difficult, seriously excruciating and relentlessly heartbreaking events that have occurred and changed our lives. Forever.

If you have recently suffered the unbearable pain of child loss, I hope and pray that this book finds you. I hope that it comforts and helps you in some small, minute way. I hope that this book will shed some light on such a sensitive topic that needs to be discussed. Our children need and deserve to be talked about. They deserve to be celebrated. It's an essential part of our grieving process and an even more essential part of our healing process. I know that I can't bring back your beloved child—if I could, I would. Unfortunately, the only thing that I can do is hope that this book will shed a little light on some of the darkest days of your life, and some of the darkest days yet to come.

Perhaps you know someone who has experienced child loss, and is suffering now. Or maybe you feel that you need more information on this "taboo" topic that is so shamelessly shunned and forgotten about by our society. I will allow myself to be a window. A window into my soul for you. For Bo.

I'm going to share our story, our journey trudging through the dark valleys and constant agony of child loss. How we walked through the darkest depth of grief that we've ever known. Together. How we were able to make it out of the other end of the tunnel. Together. And how it made us stronger than ever. But in order to fully be of help, I need to explain our story from the beginning. How our family went from the blissfulness of what felt like "Heaven" to the true depths of debilitating Hell.

The Good Old Days

My name is Amanda Hartwig, and I live in the small town of Horicon, Wisconsin. When I pictured my life years ago, I imagined three or four children. I would picture a wonderful man to call my husband, a nice home to grow old in, and spending my days as a stay at home mommy to my beautiful kids. As I got a little older, and because things don't usually go as planned, I pictured someone who would take care of my sweet daughter, Ariana Janet ("Ari"), like his own daughter.

I met my Godsend of a husband, Wayne Hartwig, Jr, in the middle of October, 2013. I believe that it was by fate that we met. I picked up my daughter Ari, from Nana Flo's house after work. While I was gathering her things to take her home, Flo stopped me a few different times to tell me that there was a really cute guy out in the garage with her husband. But I refused. I just wanted to get home and get on with our night. After some playful banter back and forth, I finally allowed Ariana to say goodbye to Flo's husband and the two friends he had over in the garage. While she was saying goodbye to the guys, I noticed a rather attractive man standing there. His big brown eyes pierced my soul. His hood was up because it was chilly outside. Even in the garage, the air had such a nip to it. I came back in the house and I was completely starstruck. I smiled and felt a little bit nervous. Something about this man had piqued an interest in me. I asked Flo what his name was, and his story. She didn't know much, but she did know that his name was Wayne and that she worked with his mother. While I packed up my vehicle and was fastening Ariana into her car seat, Wayne's friend, Kerry Bence, came hobbling over. Between his drunken slurs, he chuckled and said, "Hey Amanda! That's Wayne, and he thinks you're hot!" And while I contemplated then and there, getting in my car and driving away, something stopped me. I looked into the garage and saw Wayne standing there, shaking his head in embarrassment. I gave him my number. I didn't expect anything to ever come from it. I didn't know it then, but God had a definitive plan that was underlined beneath all of these small intricate details. Neither of us anticipated finding each other. We waited several weeks before going on our first date. We spent those weeks prior to our first date talking and texting. It felt so natural to the both of us. Our first date was around ten hours long. We went to a local zoo, out to lunch, walked around the mall, and searched for Christmas presents. Afterwards, we went out for coffee and saw a movie at a local theatre. The hours wisped by so quickly.

We hit it off perfectly and before we knew it, a few weeks later, we were in a relationship. We had the same morals and values, the same ideas for the future and we both felt such a strong, comfortable connection with each other. Nothing ever came as easy as it did with us. Wayne accepted not only me but my (then) three-year-old daughter, Ariana, as well.

In fact, by the end of November 2013, I decided that it was time for Wayne to meet Ari. We decided to go to a history museum. I watched in amazement as she opened her heart up to Wayne. She rode on top of his shoulders while we spent time looking at all of the interesting exhibits. I admired the look in his eye when he would talk to my daughter and how she would talk back with smiles. I enjoyed watching them be silly together and how they made each other laugh. I journaled about the day in Ariana's journal that I had kept for her since she was a baby.

We spent the next couple of months meeting each other's families, enjoying the holidays and spending quality time together. He showed me the ropes when it came to ice fishing, and I showed him what it meant to be a parent to a beautiful little girl.

After I first met Wayne's parents, his dad sent him a text message that said: "She's the one, over." As if he were texting on a walkie talkie.

To some, it may seem like Wayne and I moved particularly fast, but to us, the relationship just felt destined to be had. The feelings demanded to be felt.

In January 2014, Wayne and I began the stressful and ongoing process of house hunting. We spent time searching online and walked through a variety of different houses. All of which were in Horicon. We came across one with three bedrooms and fell in love with its charm. We ended up closing on our home at the end of February 2014.

On February 14, 2014, Valentine's Day, we found out that we were expecting and that we were due on October 22, 2014.

Ariana was at her dad's house for the weekend, so I asked Wayne if I could take a pregnancy test that we picked up the previous day, and he agreed. I took the test with the door open and Wayne was able to watch as the test turned positive. The second line came up on the pregnancy test; positively pregnant. I watched as the sight took Wayne's breath away. He backed out of the bathroom and grabbed his knees, slightly gasping for air, trying to process everything at once, he was in shock.

Shortly after the big baby news, Wayne made another big decision in his life. He proposed marriage to me in March, 2014.

He called and said that he had pulled a muscle in his back

getting out of the shower, and that he needed some help. On my way to the house, I contemplated calling an ambulance because I knew that, with me being pregnant, there was no way I would be able to lift him as easily as someone else could. Against my better judgment, I waited to call.

When I walked into the house, I saw the wooden staircase leading up to the second story lit up by small, white tealight candles and I couldn't help but follow them in amazement. As I turned the corner, they led me to the first bedroom door.

This was the door that would be the entrance to our sweet baby's nursery. This would be the door that I would open to wake our little bundle of joy up from his naps, and be the room that I would rock him fast asleep in. This was the door that held so many memories that were just waiting patiently to be made.

I took a breath and touched the white wooden door panel as I felt my heart beating faster and faster. I slowly opened the door to find the tealights shaped into a heart on the floor, all lit up and flaming bright. It was truly breathtaking. I looked over to see Wayne standing by the closet door, trembling. I walked over to him, still unsure of what was yet to come.

He got down on one knee.

"Amanda, we've built a great foundation and this is the room where our family is going to grow in. I love you so much, I can't wait to grow old with you, *will you marry me*?" he asked.

I was in shock and overwhelmed with the idea that someone loved me so much that he would put so much thought and effort into a single special moment.

And without hesitation, I said yes.

In our engagement photos, we had a picture of Wayne, Ariana and I holding chalkboards. Wayne's board read, "I bought a house!"

Ariana's board read, "I'm going to be a big sister!"

My chalkboard read, "I said yes!"

At this point, I remember my life in total bliss. At this point, we had it all. At this point, we had everything.

We had so much going on in such a short amount of time. And I loved every minute of it. We were planning a wedding, preparing for a baby, moving and decorating a new house, and getting Ariana ready for 4-K (four-year-old kindergarten).

Now, I am very well aware that these things normally are designed to happen in life at all different times, in many different circumstances. Even though we had constant tasks to accomplish, all the time, it never tore us apart. We thrived against these odds. It may sound crazy, but the more that we had going on, the more inseparable we became. It empowered us and made us such a strong force together.

"Heaven"

On Tuesday, October 7, 2014 at 12:27 PM, we welcomed our beautiful son **Bo William Hartwig** into the world. At three weeks early, he weighed eight pounds, five ounces and was 21 inches long. I pushed for only a matter of minutes and our sweet little boy was born into this place. And for that very moment, time stood still. Completely still. Our whole world hung on this very moment.

At. A. Complete. Halt.

We admired Bo's little hands and feet, counted his ten fingers and toes, and then counted them again. We spent what felt like hours just breathing in his smell and watching him squirm. Before I knew it, the excruciating pain that I felt from labor, blissfully whisked away and was abruptly forgotten. I remember playing, "Dare You to Move" by the band, Switchfoot, and that became somewhat of his birth song tribute.

Bo was only a couple seconds old when the doctor placed him on my chest. While lying on my chest, he picked his head up to look at us. Everyone in the room watched in amazement at how strong this little human was. He had defined muscles and hardly any fat on his little body. He reminded us of a miniature body builder that was ready to take on anything that this world had in store for him.

He was absolutely perfect; Bo was absolutely beautiful.

This moment, this moment right here is what we like to call *Heaven on Earth*.

From this moment, our world was inevitably changed, for the better.

Yes, there were many sleepless nights. There were countless moments of exhaustion between Wayne and me. From his very first night home, Bo had his days and nights mixed up. I breastfed him for about three weeks and then made the transition to formula. He spent the first couple months of his life in complete colic.

Webster's Dictionary defines colic as *a sharp sudden pain in the stomach: a physical condition in which a baby is very uncomfortable and cries for long periods of time.*

Bo's poor little tummy didn't agree with the transition to the formula that we had switched him to. And these sleepless nights led to a little bit of a struggle in regards to Wayne and me, but we muscled through them. The only thing that would ever give him a little bit of relief is Gripe Water. Prior to Bo having colic, I never knew that this amazing magic potion existed for infants. It was a Godsend in those stressful moments where nothing would help and the feelings of defeat set in.

About one month after we brought Bo home, I realized that I was struggling with postpartum depression. Actually, to be completely honest, Wayne realized it. Although I had everything I had ever wanted, I was still struggling with stress and the pressure to be a mommy to two beautiful children.

Wayne would often take the brunt of my anger when I would lash out, uncontrollably. I became so easily overwhelmed with daily household chores like washing the dishes and vacuuming. I went from zero to one hundred in a split second. In the blink of an eye, if I wasn't yelling or upset, I was crying and hysterical. Things that were tiny issues, magically transformed into massive mountains that I created all in my own mind. But with Wayne's full support, I went to the doctor.

The doctor explained that this is a very **common** struggle with mothers after they give birth. My hormones had a chemical imbalance and a pill was supposed to correct it. He assured me that it was going to be okay. We left the doctor's office and decided to start the prescription that night. Within one week, I felt a huge difference. Wayne saw a difference. I was a joy to be around again.

Life was definitely an adjustment when Bo came. Although it took a little while to get some minor things like my mood swings figured out, we eventually started to learn how to maneuver another chapter of our life together.

If you think that you are struggling with postpartum depression, don't wait. Go in to see your doctor and be honest about your feelings. I promise you that you're not the only one who feels this way, even though it feels very alienating.

Bo loved a lot of things, but he especially loved his big sister. From the first moment that Ari held him, it was evident that her heart opened up, immediately.

The second time Ari held Bo, he farted on her, and as she laughed, she said, "Okay, that's enough." And handed him back to us.

We had a good amount of anxiety, which is normal for new parents. When Wayne and I got enough courage to take Bo out in public, we were at a local store in West Bend, Wisconsin.

We weren't in the store but twenty minutes when Ari asked, "Daddy, do you know what that yucky smell is?"

Wayne and I both looked at each other apprehensively, and then looked down at Bo in his stroller.

We realized that he pooped. But not just any kind of poop. This was an all-out explosive "doo-doo." A blow out of the diaper, oozing through his pants, out of this world kind of predicament.

Parents that are reading this with children, you probably know what I'm talking about!

We found a family bathroom at the front of the store and abandoned our cart and stroller as we all quickly rushed into the bathroom to evaluate the current situation. Of course, since this was the first adventure out of the house since Bo's arrival, he was wearing an adorable Carhartt outfit with blue jean overalls.

Wayne was about a quarter of the way finished with changing his diaper when Bo decided to start to wiggle. And of course, it wasn't just any sort of wiggle. This was the type of wiggle that looked like a shimmy. You know, when you have an itch on your butt, or you're trying to fit into that old pair of jeans that haven't fit since college. And due to his shimmy wiggle and the amount of fecal matter, the poop didn't stay in his diaper at all. No, it decided to waltz up his back like it had somewhere else to be.

Before we knew it, we had poop on the walls of the bathroom, the changing table, on the floor, in Bo's hair, and all over us. All we could do was laugh. I quickly ran out to grab a plastic shopping bag because the poop was so bad that Bo's outfit needed to be changed. We decided at that moment to go home. Our very first day out with a newborn was a disaster.

It was an absolute disaster. A beautiful, imperfect disaster.

A disaster that we cherish only as a memory now.

As Bo grew older, he and his sister became more and more inseparable. She was there for every milestone in his life. I can't think of a memory with Bo that doesn't have Ari in it. Every time that Bo would smile, it would be because of her. She was always making him laugh. And when you would look into his eyes while he was looking at her, you could almost see the pure, unconditional love that he had for her. It was like she was the only person in the world and to Bo, she was. The light of his life. He started to roll over and Ari cheered him on. When Bo started to crawl, she would be on her hands and knees right alongside of him.

The kids both had a homebased teacher who would come over weekly to visit for an hour. She would go over many different educational things like reading, playing with toys, tips and ways to help Wayne and me be more involved. One of the times that she came over, we had an activity where Ariana had to bounce colorful balls outside into an umbrella that was tipped upside down. For some reason, every time that Ari would throw a ball into the umbrella, Bo would laugh hysterically. He would laugh so hard that it would make the three of us laugh at and with him. It was spectacular silliness that lasted an amazing amount of time. Hilarious side note, Ari laughed so hard at Bo that she actually peed her pants. These are the moments when time stood still for us. These are the moments that we continue to treasure now. Being able to watch Bo and Ari together was a beloved gift. They had an inseparable bond that was undeniable since the day that they met. Over the next passing months, we would find so much enjoyment from watching the two of them chase each other all over the living room floor. Bo would be interested in any toy that Ariana was playing with, so he would crawl over to her and try to get it, and Ari would let him. Then she would crawl slowly towards him to try to get it back and Bo would speed crawl over to the couch and pull himself up and reach for me, as if I could save him from being chased. He did the same thing when Wayne would be on the floor playing with the kids. Anytime that he was being chased, his safe place was in my arms.

Bo had the most contagious laugh. A whole, full belly laugh. A laugh that would use all of your stomach and shoulder muscles. One that would make you cry because you were laughing so hard. A true, authentic, one of a kind baby giggle. A laugh that was a form of music to your ears. That was his. A chuckle that was Bo's, I can just hear it now. He exuberated love. Pure, authentic and relentless love. The kind of love that you can only dream about. That same love that only a select few people ever get to experience.

And we were one of the blessed people that got to experience such perfection. We would be in the supermarket and I would be minding my own business getting groceries, and complete strangers would stop and tell me how beautiful of a baby I had. Oftentimes I wouldn't know how to respond other than a quick, "Thank you!" He would sit in the top of the cart and smile at everyone. And I must admit I was more socially awkward, so anytime that he would smile at people it would force me to talk to them.

Bo kept growing. Blossoming into such a strong, goofy little boy. My favorite pastime with Bo was when we would sit on the front porch steps and watch the cars pass by. We would look for school buses and police cars. Sometimes even firetrucks would pass by. He would be fascinated by the colors of nature, the grass and trees. Sometimes when people would walk by, we would stop and have little conversations because Bo would have such a friendly demeanor about him.

We would often spend time outside once Ari and Wayne returned home too. We would go on walks all over our little town, play at parks and play ball in the front yard. We loved to spend time together, and it seemed to come so easily.

Wayne and I thought that we had parenting down pat. We had a well ironed out routine and a nice schedule in place where we would do bath time with Bo together. Both Wayne and I would wash him and watch him play in the bath water. That was our family time. We would double team getting him out of the bath and into pajamas. If Ari was home with us, she would be so happy to help make him giggle by putting her hair in his face while he laid on the floor to get dried off.

I can recall the smell of the Johnson and Johnson lavender baby lotion that we would always put on Bo after his baths. It would make him smell so good, and he loved his lotion. I would always blow hot air onto my hands in an effort to help protect him from the cold. We would brush his little hair and spike it up into a mohawk. Although, we called it a "Bo-hawk."

In Bo's short little life on earth, he got to do so many different things. He got to take pictures with many turkeys, feed giraffes and pet deer at a local zoo. Bo went fishing with his daddy and papa, and caught many fish. He was on television because he was so cute. He had a love for chocolate milk, his blue shark blanket, Mickey Mouse, balloons and his favorite, Grandma Pookers. Bo and his grandma had such a special relationship. They were so close and shared an unbreakable bond. If Bo wasn't with me, he was almost always with his Grandma.

I felt so blessed to be able to spend his entire life with him. Bo was never in daycare because I was a stay at home mom. There were days where I would be doing dishes in the kitchen, dancing and singing songs. His favorites were "Sangria" by Blake Shelton and "Wagon Wheel" by Darius Rucker. Bo would laugh at me dancing around like a goofball, while he sat in his highchair and watched. He would clap along with me, and we would be silly together. If we weren't dancing goofy in the kitchen, then we were doing the Hot Dog dance and watching *Mickey Mouse Clubhouse* on the Disney channel.

The months seemed to fly by. We set a wedding date of May 24, 2015, which gave us a little over a year to plan the big day. I remember being pregnant and spending so much of my energy on the littlest details for the wedding.

The wedding happened at a beautiful hunting club that had a sophisticated, rustic feel. Wayne's uncle sang, "A Thousand Years" by Christina Perry as I walked down the aisle. And he sang it beautifully. He also sang the song, "Yellow" by Coldplay, which the wedding party walked down to. We had a beautiful sand ceremony where we had yellow, white, gray and blue sand in separate vases. Ariana and Bo came up and, as a family, we took turns blending the sand together into a bigger vase.

The yellow sand represented Ari because she brought the love and sunshine to our home. The blue sand represented Bo because he was full of innocence, silliness, and little boy things. The gray sand represented Wayne because of his amazing hard work, loyalty and dedication to his family. And the white sand represented myself, being the glue of the family. I tried my hardest to make sure that everything was absolutely perfect, and it was. It really was.

Shortly after Wayne and I were married, we were expecting our third child. Our wedding night baby! Bo would so often sit on my lap while on the couch, and kiss my belly when I would say, "Kiss the baby!" He would open his mouth all the way and give a big wet kiss to my stomach. He loved his baby sibling so much, so quickly. And it showed.

One night, Wayne was in the kitchen and I came in with Bo on my hip. In regards to our third child, I said, "I don't think I want another boy; I have my boy, we need a girl!"

Little did I know that this moment would stick with me for the rest of my life. How could I have said that? How come I didn't know what was coming for us? Did I "jinx" it? Did I say something wrong? I couldn't help but carry this guilt around with me, because my mind would go through all sorts of unnecessary scenarios that didn't really make any logical sense.

The Shadow of Death

Thursday September 3, 2015, was a day like any other. Bo William had been crawling around and getting into mischief all day long. He had always been a busy worker bee, or at least that's what I would always call him. He was someone who always needed to stay busy and explore. He explored EVERYTHING. We would push all the furniture together so we could corral him into one area, otherwise we would be running all over the house. It was our own, make shift play pen. His favorite spot was in the living room. He loved to sit on our rustic floor rug, and play with blocks, books or whatever his big sister had for toys. He was only ten months old, soon to be eleven months. And he always had a smile on his face and he carried so much love in his heart. He was so happy, and today was no different.

When Wayne came home around 4:00 PM, I realized that Bo had been slightly warm for a couple of hours. I assumed it was because it was 90 degrees outside and he was generally just a warmer baby, I didn't have much to worry about. I didn't think much of it as he didn't show it affected him in any way. I talked to Wayne and we both decided that we would give him some infants Advil to help the fever break.

Our little Bo started teething at a very young age. He had eight teeth by the time he was nine months old. His one-year molars were on their way in and that's what we chalked his fever up to being caused by. Since Bo acted normal, we never even gave it a second thought. Bo took his medicine; he never had a problem taking Advil. I honestly think that he enjoyed the taste of it because he would lean in and open his mouth every time that I brought the syringe near.

That night, Bo kissed both of us goodnight and he went to bed with a smile on his face.

The feeling that I felt the next morning when I woke up was indescribable. I woke up and looked at our monitor and Bo was lying in the exact same position that he was in the night before. Immediately, horror shot through me. The feeling was unbearable.

Somewhere deep in my heart, I knew.

But I went about my normal morning routine, being in complete denial.

I woke Ariana up for school and put her clothes in the bathroom for her to get dressed. Just like I did every day.

It was when she shut the bathroom door that I opened his.

The same door that we had gone through hundreds of times.

The same door that I stared at while Wayne asked me to marry him.

I opened his door and peered into the darkness.

It was quiet.

And still.

I tiptoed to Bo's crib and leaned over.

Believing that he was "here," sleeping peacefully.

Believing that it was me just overreacting to my anxiety and horrible thoughts, always thinking the worst.

I rubbed his clothes and tapped him gently.

He was stiff.

He was cold.

He was so cold.

For a split second I thought that he was sleeping so hard that he just needed to be tapped a little more.

It wasn't until my fingers brushed up against his skin that I knew.

I saw his body shift all at once.

He was stiff.

I reached in with both hands to pick him up and turn him towards me.

It was still dark in the room, but I could see his skin wasn't normal.

He didn't look the same.

I ran to the light, with him in my arms.

I looked down and saw him.

Disproportioned due to the lack of oxygen.

All I could do was cry.

"Oh, Bo," I uttered, in tears.

I turned the light on and sat on the carpet in his room, with him in my arms.

Without thinking, I called his dad.

All I could feel was his freezing cold body against me, and I was hanging onto every ring of that phone call.

I heard him answer and I screamed, "COME HOME NOW!" and hung up.

I called 911 franticly.

I had to mutter words to the operator, "My…son isn't… breathing."

I somehow hoped that she would put me in the right mindset to save his life.

She said calmly, "We need to start CPR immediately; do you know how to do this?"

My mind was scrambling back to every textbook I've read and every first aid class that I've ever taken. I screamed out "NO!" in horror and she calmly said, "Okay, you're going to have to open his mouth by pulling his chin down."

I shrieked in horror.

Looking down at his face with the lights on now, I saw him.

His purple and blue pigment.

His nose dented in towards the right.

His lifeless body sleeping his soundest sleep.

I laid him on the rug in the middle of his room.

I lifted his bottom lip open.

I heard the voice on the other end of the phone say, "You're going to need to breathe a small breath in, as small as a puff of air." I took a deep breath.

Thinking in my mind of what a small breath of air actually was, and praying that I would do it correctly so that my baby would wake up.

The moment that I felt my lips meet his, all I could see was my life flashing before my eyes.

I could see his life flashing before my eyes.

His body was so cold.

His lips that once gave me warm, drool-filled kisses, were now stiff.

They weren't moving.

Nothing on him moved.

His hands and feet were still stiff and in the position that I found him in on his belly in the crib.

I puffed a breath of air and I felt my air go into his mouth and into his little lungs.

She told me to press on his chest several times. I repeated this process three more times.

And then, after the third pump on his small chest, I thought, "My husband always locks the front door!"

I panicked, full of tears I screamed that the door was locked.

She instructed me to run and unlock it and return immediately.

I did just that. Tripping down the stairs, unlocking the door.

I rushed back upstairs and grabbed his bottom lip again.

Just as I finished breathing into his lungs, I heard the bathroom door open.

"Mommy, what's going on? What's happening to Bo-Bo?"

I looked up in horror, and without skipping a beat, I screamed, "GET BACK IN THAT BATHROOM NOW AND SHUT THE DOOR!"

As I continued to do compressions on his little chest, I screamed to the dispatcher, "I need someone here NOW, right now!!"

She replied so calmly, "I know that it feels like a really long time but it's only been a couple of minutes, they're coming as fast as they can, I promise, but right now, Amanda, I need you to breathe into his mouth again."

I grabbed his chin to pull his bottom lip back, while tears ran down my face.

I puffed another breath of air into his tiny little body.

In that moment, I remembered the song from when Bo was first born, "Dare You to Move" by Switchfoot.

"I dare you to lift yourself off of the floor."

I was begging and pleading for him to move.

For Bo to breathe.

I searched for his tiny breaths as I continued CPR.

And then I heard it.

I heard the front door open.

I didn't care who was coming in, I just knew that someone was coming to help me escape this nightmare.

The first responder was climbing up the stairs as I was doing compressions.

He came in and checked his pulse.

He scooped him up delicately from the carpet and headed down the stairs.

I peeled myself up and followed right behind them.

There was no ambulance, no other help yet.

He laid Bo down on the porch rug and pressed down on his chest multiple times.

He did compressions on my son, right on the front porch of our home. And I hit my knees and watched.

Another first responder arrived and grabbed a white tube that was connected to a bag that she held over my son's mouth and nose to push the air into his lungs.

"PLEASE SAVE MY BABY!" I screamed.

I hurdled into uncontrollable agony.

While on the floor, I threw my hands down and begged.

I pleaded. I prayed. Whatever that was.

"Please…Please…Please!" I said over and over.

In the middle of hyperventilating, I called my mother-in-law. Barely being able to make out the numbers because of the tears in my eyes. Barely able to push the buttons because of the adrenaline coursing through my veins.

I heard her pick up the phone and screamed, "GET OVER HERE NOW."

And without thinking, I hung up the phone.

While I was on my knees, I was close enough to the floor to be level with my Bo's body.

His little body fit perfectly on the rug that we had on the porch.

His little body that was still so stiff.

He was still in the same position that I found him in minutes prior.

His limbs were stiff, although they would move slightly with each compression.

His body that I wished so desperately would start to move on its own.

I kept my eyes on Bo's chest and waited for him to gasp for air.

I watched his mouth to see if it would open and close without help.

I watched his eyes to see if they would open.

I studied him like a test that I wish I would have been prepared for.

I prayed.

I begged in my mind, over and over.

"I'll switch places with him, just save him and take me. I will go!" I thought to myself.

All the while, I was screaming and crying hysterically.

Finally, I saw the ambulance in my peripheral vision, and I heard the sirens.

And yet, my eyes were fixed on him.

I watched his chest go up and down with the hands of the first responder.

I watched the woman squeeze the air into his lungs with the little mouth piece.

They both picked him up and carried him towards the ambulance.

It seemed like a split second went by and the ambulance started moving.

I started running towards it, but the lights went on and it took off.

I knew it was hospital bound.

But in the back of my mind I knew that my husband was still on his way home and that he would arrive at any moment, and that we would be right behind that ambulance.

I tried not to panic.

I told myself that he would be okay.

I told myself that I did what I could, and that it was enough.

At this point, there was a police officer at the house, I'm not quite sure when he arrived. He may or may not have been there the entire time.

I didn't really recognize him until the ambulance drove off. I just sobbed and hoped that my husband would get home as fast as he could.

I recall the officer telling me that I had a daughter that I needed to check on, but I couldn't get anything to register in my mind.

I couldn't function at all. I couldn't move.

One of the first responders that my daughter knew already went up to check on her.

He picked her up and brought her downstairs.

I grabbed onto her and held her tightly.

She looked up at me with tears in her eyes.

I told her that I had to leave to go to the hospital and that her grandma would be here shortly.

The first responder stayed with her until my mother-in-law got there.

Ariana, my five-year-old, innocent daughter cried for her baby brother.

All I could think of was *what did she see? What did she hear? Did she see him like this?*

Finally, my husband pulled up.

"What the Hell is happening?" he asked, walking quickly toward me.

Little did I know, he had driven by the ambulance with the lights on.

I shook my head no and told him that we needed to get to the hospital.

The police officer offered to take us there as fast as possible.

I remember the entire ride there; it was foggy and the conditions were terrible. I replayed Bo in my mind, over and over. The way his face looked, the colors of his skin and the bitter coldness of his body. Was that my son? Was this really happening? Was this a dream? Could I wake up?

In my heart, I was beyond devastated. Devastated doesn't even begin to cover it. I was broken.

I replayed doing CPR. I prayed that I did enough to save him. I prayed that they were doing all that they could to save him.

When we arrived at the hospital, we went through the double doors of the Emergency Room. We checked in and they let us back to the emergency department.

As we turned the corner to the right, groups of nurses and a doctor stood waiting in the hallway. Some with tears in their eyes, and some with their heads down. I looked at the doctor as she started to shake her head *no*. I remember grabbing her arm and begging her to do something. I refused to take no for an answer.

I saw Bo lying on the hospital bed and approached his bedside as I took in the whole picture. Wayne was on his knees down toward the left of Bo. Our baby lying there with his blue pajamas cut right in half, off of his body. He was attached to a machine that read his heart and what should have been his pulse.

And there was a woman standing over him concentrating on his compressions and counting.

Walking up to Bo felt surreal.

The doctor was quick to say, "STOP" to the woman doing compressions.

I looked at her, and while she was looking back at me, I quickly said, "Keep going!"

The machine needed to take an accurate reading on his pulse.

He didn't have one. But no one could touch him.

I started to breathe faster and shallow. A nurse grabbed my arm and had me sit.

I looked up and saw my husband next to me. I looked at the doctor and watched as she shut the machine down.

In disbelief, I felt so frustrated. I looked down and there Bo was.

He had pigment back in his cheeks. He wasn't purple or blue anymore. His nose wasn't indented. Wayne and I hurled ourselves over him. Feeling how cold he still was. We were in denial and shocked at what was happening. It didn't seem real.

I still to this day wish that I would have picked him up.

The last time I held my baby was when I found him in his crib.

I didn't hold him at the hospital.

Not once. And I have no idea why.

He just lay there.

We laid on top of him crying.

I laid my head on his chest and felt the cold.

I kissed him on his cheeks, his forehead and his hands.

He looked like he was fast asleep.

The deepest sleep of his life.

Meanwhile, we felt like our hearts were literally being ripped out of our chest.

In excruciating, indescribable pain.

We felt like we were dying too.

How can this amazing, perfect little boy with so much left to do and so much left to see and offer to this world be here?

How could he just be gone?

Just then, Wayne Sr. stormed into the ER with tears in his eyes.

He yelled, **"Lord, we don't know why this is happening. But we need You. We don't know why Bo's gone but let Your will be done!"**

Immediately, I felt anger. Such relentless anger.

How could I need anyone that would take away my child?

How could I need someone that is putting me through this?

I don't need anyone. Or anything.

I just need my son to breathe again!

I happened to look up, and saw a nurse hanging her head over my husband's shoulder.

I realized that it was Wayne Jr's cousin, who had just seen us months prior, at our wedding.

Our wedding, four months previous to this, when Bo was dancing with all of the ladies.

When we had pure bliss.

And just like that we were bombarded with questions.

Do you want to donate his organs?

Do you have a reverend that you want us to call?

Do you have family that you need to notify?

And then we met PJ, who was the Dodge County medical examiner.

PJ stated, "It's mandatory for children under two years old to have an autopsy done, I'm going to need you to stop touching and kissing him."

As soon as he said that we were no longer able to kiss Bo's face, Wayne and I both looked at each other. I knew he was only following his protocol, but, immediately, I felt so protective over my son. I started to get snippy with him because I wasn't going to stop holding him close to me. I didn't want to stop kissing his beautiful cheeks.

He said, "I just need to ask you a few questions."

And without skipping a beat, I quickly said, "Then ask them! But I'm going to continue loving my baby."

His questions were more about organ donations, and "our versions" of what happened the previous night.

So many questions and interrogations. On the worst day of our lives, we felt so criminalized. Not only criminalized, but forcefully rushed.

Due to the amount of sick people in the world that murder their children, our last moments were cut short because they needed to do an investigation.

Bo needed to have an autopsy done. It was a requirement. But still, I couldn't bear to think of my baby being cut open with a scalpel. It made me physically sick to my stomach.

Time blurred together and eventually we had to leave the hospital. That was the worst part.

We were completely empty-handed.

Wayne's dad drove us home. Where we were met by a police officer standing guard in front of Bo's room, making sure that nothing was shifted or moved around.

Nothing could be touched. Nothing could be moved.

While my mother-in-law was here watching Ariana and sending her to school, she was trying desperately to keep herself busy and to be positive, so she went into Bo's room to grab the bottle that he was put to bed with the previous night.

The cop scolded her and told her to put it back. It was going to be collected into evidence, eventually.

We weren't allowed to go in until the coroner arrived. He arrived with his colleague in tow.

"We are going to go upstairs and set up a camera with a baby doll. You are going to need to explain and show in detail, to the best of your ability, what happened to Bo," PJ said.

Wayne and I were in awe. We looked at each other and our mouths dropped. We felt like we did so much wrong already, and here we were being criminalized.

Wayne went up first, because he was the one that put Bo to bed the night before. He showed the medical examiners how he held him up above his head like *The Lion King*, just as he did every night. And how he laid him down in his crib on his back.

Then they called me up,

I inched up the stairs.

As I felt the diarrhea in my stomach start to gurgle.

I saw the threshold of Bo's room.

Breaking down, Wayne came to my aid.

I couldn't speak. I whimpered out in pain.

Excruciating, rip-my-heart-out type of pain.

I walked right past the middle of the room, past the rug on the floor where I gave him CPR, just hours prior.

I could barely stand, peering over that crib, the same way I did in the morning.

I saw the baby doll and panicked.

Everything came rushing back, all at once.

Everything was recorded. The iPad was in my face.

My cries, my shrieks and my inability to speak words.

Just empty cries.

I was instructed to show them how I found Bo.

I looked over the crib rail.

I saw the baby doll lying there.

I quickly showed the medical examiners the position that I found him in.

Facing down toward the crib mattress.

I picked the baby doll up the same way that I picked Bo up that morning.

I turned the doll around and I froze.

I saw Bo's face, black and blue. I was back in that moment.

I screamed, and shook my head no; I couldn't show them how I did CPR.

I was crying so hard and deeply that I struggled to breathe, I just needed the nightmare to end.

If you have never experienced the death of your child, the only way that I could even try to describe the pain of the tears that came, is that pain that comes when you have a big lump in your throat, and that lump turns into a tumor. And that same tumor birthed knives, bone spurs and gunshots.

And those gunshots trickled all the way down to the center of your heart.

And those gunshots decided to make a home there, slowly dismantling all of the heart and love that you have ever known.

The four of us came downstairs. We needed to explain to PJ that we felt so criminalized through all of this. He did his best to console us. We talked for a few more minutes, and then they had to leave to help with Bo's autopsy. And report their findings.

We live in a world where innocent parents that experience the death of their child, on the worst day of their lives, need to prove their innocence.

Looking back, PJ was just doing his job. He has one of the *hardest* jobs on this planet. And he handled the situation the best way that he possibly could have.

The Aftershock

After everything happened on Friday, September 4, 2015, we were numb from the shock. That night, we decided to stay at Wayne's parent's house for the weekend. Because the idea of coming back to our home was beyond devastating. I physically couldn't bear it. We couldn't breathe when we walked in the doorway. All the, once happy, memories had turned black and were overshadowed by the horror that took place just hours before.

I told Wayne that we were going to have to sell the house and move somewhere else. We walked in the doorway and all I could see was horrible images of the events that the house held earlier that day. All I could see was heartbreak. We were reliving the nightmare—I was reliving the nightmare. The house was covered in pure sadness and devastation.

In my mind, I heard the awful screams of desperation I made to the 911 operator; I heard and saw all the begging and groveling that I did on the floor of the doorway with the first responders, desperately hoping that they would save Bo. I saw images of him, everywhere. I felt my heart grasp for any good that was left, but I was reaching in the dark. There was nothing. It was painted black with all of the sadness, grief and overwhelming pain. We gathered whatever we could grab in our hands and got out of the house as fast as possible.

The night brought pure exhaustion; our bodies shut down and somehow fell asleep. We were in complete shock and we didn't even think that sleep was possible at that point. I recall waking up and turning to Wayne asking if it was all a bad dream, and if Bo was there. He shook his head no. We both realized he was gone and cried all over again, and again some more.

Bo died on the Friday of Labor Day weekend, which was very difficult because everything was closed on Monday. I tried calling grief places in nearby counties, the hospital that Bo was pronounced dead at, everywhere. I called anywhere that had a dial tone. But no one would answer. I left numerous voicemails. Our once bliss filled lives were hanging by threads. A loss of this magnitude, how were we going to survive this? In the matter of a few days, all the happiness that we felt completely vanished. It was only because we had a few select child loss parents that reached out to us that we were able to get through the first few days. We didn't know them, but through the conversations, they were able to explain exactly how we were feeling. They knew how it felt because they had gone through it too. And that's all that we needed to hear in those immediately fragile moments. We needed a sense of hope to be able to get through this. We needed a strong sense of hope to survive this.

A few days after Bo's death, I woke up in the middle of the night in complete horror. I screamed at the top of my lungs, and Wayne grabbed me and held on to calm me down. I tried my best to explain what I saw. It was dark, and all I saw was a crib. The crib had a set of lungs in it. No body, just lungs. A pair of Mickey Mouse hands appeared and pointed directly to the lungs, and I heard the words, "upper respiratory system" whispered. Wayne told me that I needed to write about it in Bo's baby journal.

The following days were a complete blur, even now. Trying to recall any funeral planning and arrangements is nearly impossible. I do know that our funeral director, Dan Koepsell, made most of the decisions for us. Because we were in no shape to do so. How do you plan a funeral for your child? What do you choose? Dan said that he would make Bo proud, and he was confident in saying that. He chose the floral arrangements and the Mickey Mouse that was sitting on top of his gorgeous white casket. He helped us choose a casket and held onto us as we sobbed in his office. We experienced this traumatic, surreal life altering chapter, together. And he made us feel like we weren't alone. To this very day, we are so grateful that we chose Koepsell-Murray Funeral Homes for making the decisions that we couldn't make in those fragile times.

Bo's Funeral

We had Bo's funeral on Monday, September 7, 2015. It was Bo's 11 month "Birthday." Just one short month later, on October 7th, he would have been one year old. The funeral was held at a local church, Sacred Heart Catholic Church. Wayne and I planned to have a private viewing for us to say goodbye to him. Shortly after that it would be open to our immediate family for them to say goodbye, as well.

As soon as we walked into the first doors of the church, I fell to the floor. I saw my son's little white casket sitting so peacefully at the end of the altar and I couldn't bear it. I don't even remember how I made it down the aisle to him, maybe I crawled, I don't know.

I can recall touching Bo's face and feeling the cold bitterness of his skin. He looked like himself, as if he was in the most peaceful sleep that he had ever taken. He was in his jean overalls that had a Mickey Mouse on the front with a white long sleeve shirt underneath. It was the outfit that his grandma had already purchased for his first birthday. His hair was styled in his usual Bo-hawk. That's exactly how it was when he would wake up from his naps. He smelled so differently though, he smelled like the funeral home. I can remember the smell of the embalming and the makeup. He didn't smell like himself. It didn't matter, though, I knew that's where my baby was and that's where I sat. The funeral director brought me a chair and I sat near the edge of his casket.

I remember Wayne standing over me, I could feel his tears hit the top of my head. We cried. We sobbed. It was so unreal and shocking to take in.

I wasn't sure if I was going to let Ariana see Bo. I was fearful that it would scar her for life. I didn't want her to remember her sweet little brother like that. Fr. Mike actually gave us some great advice and said that children have the best intuition when it comes to death and funerals. If she can handle it, she would, and if she couldn't then she wouldn't go up to the front. I knew that my daughter would, though. She's so brave. Her dad brought her to the funeral and stayed back while Wayne and I asked her if she wanted to see Bo one last time. She shook her head yes. And we took her to the front. She was in Wayne's arms and saw Bo lying there so peacefully. She turned into Wayne's chest and cried. She always called him her Bo-Bo. As her tears started to fall onto Wayne's shirt, I heard her call out for her brother. The connection that these two had was unlike anything that I've ever seen before. We set her on the chair that was in front of his casket. She stood up and reached in. She brushed her tiny hand across his forehead and we watched as her face showed disbelief. She pulled back abruptly. "He's so cold," she said.

We didn't know how to respond to her.

"That happens," Wayne said hesitantly.

Ari reached for Wayne and he picked her back up. She put a stuffed dog that her dad and stepmom got two of, one that could go in Bo's casket, and one for her to keep, next to his little body. Tears streamed down her tiny, delicate face. Her innocence was completely severed.

Our family was waiting in the back of the church, so we gave permission for them to come and see Bo one last time. I remember my little brother, Aaron, putting a little toy elephant in his casket.

Before the funereal, we had invited everyone to write letters that they could place in his casket.

Wayne and I decided that we wanted to say goodbye alone once more before they closed his casket. We gave him our kisses and told him that we loved him so much. I kissed him before we walked away and nodded at Dan, the funeral director, to close his casket for us.

That would be the very last time that I would ever kiss, touch, or see my baby boy.

It wasn't until Bo's visitation that I felt something hit me, maybe it was pure and utter exhaustion. I must have given 200 hugs. Only a few select people could bring themselves to stay through the entire service. Some people couldn't even make it down the aisle to Bo. They saw my sweet son's casket and couldn't bear to come through the visitation line. Some paid their respects to everyone down the aisle and some only paid their respects to Wayne and me, as Bo's parents. Some people didn't know what to say so they just shook their heads, I honestly preferred it that way. Some said that God was holding him now and that He needed another angel. That was honestly tough to hear. It was tough to hear because all I needed was him here with me. Some commented on how wiped out we looked. It was heart wrenching. Wayne and I were in a complete state of shock. We were shocked at the reality that was in front of us.

I recall feeling dizzy, as if the hugs took every ounce of my energy and I didn't have any left to stand. I sat down every chance that I could. I was 18 weeks pregnant with our third child, but I couldn't even think of the baby inside me. And that carried the burden of guilt within itself.

The ridiculous things that people decide are acceptable to say when you have your child's funeral is crazy. Even the days following the funeral. It has been my experience that people lack a huge amount of empathy with child death, in general.

We were asked what happened to Bo, and we were told that divorce rates double after a child dies in the home, all while in the visitation line at his funeral. His casket was on the other side of where I was standing.

If you have experienced the stupid things that people say, I'm so sorry. Know that they don't mean it, and if they do, they don't deserve you or your beautiful family. Find people who love and support your healing process. In whatever way that is.

Please know that you are not alone.

As I turned to admire his white casket again, I thought about how my other baby, in Heaven, was physically lying to my right side. He was in a place that I never thought I would see him. Not in my millions of worst nightmares. My heart broke every time I looked toward his casket and saw the big photo of him on top of it. All I could think of was, "Why is this happening? Why my son? WHY MY BABY?"

We wanted to give Bo the best funeral service that we possibly could. We wanted to celebrate his life. Even though it was brief, and so unfair to us and him, we knew that he deserved the absolute best. And that's exactly what we tried to give him.

During the service, Wayne and I decided to stand up in front of everyone and explain exactly who Bo William was to us, and how much he IS loved. I told Wayne before his funeral even started that I was going to get through our speech, no matter what it took. I was going to do it for Bo, no matter how long it took. As we approached the podium, I felt my breathing become more rapid, I scrambled fast to find whatever courage I had so that I could speak out to everyone.

"Not in a million years did I think that I would ever be up here looking out at all of you for this reason. I speak for my husband and myself; we love each and every one of you for showing your love and support for our son. Wayne and I are grieving deeply, the pain is completely evident and this wound we have hurts incredibly. Bo passed away unexpectedly, asleep, in his crib on September 4th, a day in our family that will forever remain a day from Hell.

Bo would have been eleven months old today. We were busy planning his first birthday party and looking forward to Christmas this year. To each of you who knew him personally, he loved you, he loved everyone. To the people that are here that weren't blessed with our son's presence, you would have loved and been smitten by him. He had a way with winning hearts over. He was an amazing, spunky, mischievous little boy who always had a smile on his face. Hearing his laugh would make you smile. Hearing him say 'deer,' point, and jump was a sign that he was going to be a hunter. He enjoyed the outdoors, just like his daddy. Watching him focus on the next obstacle and to see that determination in his eyes to see what he was going to accomplish next was simply amazing and exciting for us to watch as his parents. We're so grateful for the time that we got to spend with our Bo. He blessed our lives, our home and our hearts every day. Hearing him say "dada" or "ma" is something that we long for deeply.

One specific memory that I have of Bo is when we took our annual Hartwig vacation up north, and we went to a petting zoo. They had deer that could be handfed and Bo jumped at the opportunity. Seeing Wayne and Bo walk up to this mama doe was breathtaking, but seeing Bo's reaction when he reached out and pet her head, and rubbed her ears was priceless.

A more recent, mischievous memory I have of our son is when I laid him down for a nap during the day. About a half hour later, I checked on him and he had managed to get his pants and diaper off. The problem was that the diaper had poop in it. That poop was then spread all over his crib, on his hands, his chin, and bedding. His poop was everywhere. I walked in his room and he smiled, and did his little giggle that he did. He kept us on our toes, to say the least.

Watching Bo with his big sister, Ariana, is something that I will never forget. Ari and Bo would sit on the floor and pass a ball back and forth. They would chase each other and kiss each other all the time. He would light up when he saw his sister. Wayne and I would often spend nights just watching them goof around in the living room together.

Grieving is tremendously hard, exhausting and a difficult thing to process. At first, we cursed God; I told him that he made a mistake by taking our son. To be honest, we still feel this way. He was an angel to this world, someone who was going to make a difference and someone who left way too soon! Wayne and I feel as though we were robbed. But these children really are gifts. Gifts from Him, and He allows us to have them and it is Him who decides when they are called home. We know that every day will be a constant battle to rid the hate and rage out of our hearts, but it has to be done. We also know that we have the love of our family and friends, our community and our parish to help us through this unimaginable nightmare. We can't imagine this pain ever subsiding, but rather strengthening us so that we make it through each day.

Bo doesn't hurt at all right now. He didn't hurt when he left this place. He was already at peace when I found him. But now, he's in the arms of our grandparents and they're rocking him right to sleep. So instead of mourning his passing, I ask each of you to hug and hold your little ones, because we are not guaranteed tomorrow. For us, and for Bo, tomorrow will come when our day is done at this place. When we die, and we can be reunited. Wayne and I will pick up right where we left off; we will raise him and feel his touch, hear his laugh and see his smile again. We miss you Bo, we miss your hugs and your wet kisses. Mommy and daddy love you so much and would give anything to have you back. We are going to remember you each and every day. We will let your life live on through ours. We promise to not let anyone forget you, especially your siblings."

I looked out at everyone, making eye contact with Ariana who was snuggled up next to her dad in the crowd, then took a big breath and said, "Twinkle, twinkle little star, up in Heaven is where you are, flying high and twinkling bright, my guiding star, my shining light. Twinkle, twinkle little star, my perfect Angel is what you are."

After I finished speaking, Wayne and I headed to our seats at the front of the church. We couldn't take our eyes off of Bo's beautiful casket. My heart felt as if someone was preforming an open-heart surgery on me. The rest of the service went on and, to be honest, I can't remember most of it. The priest told the rest of the people at the service that his burial would be for immediate family only. And everyone complied.

After the funeral, we decided that it was time to go back to our home again. And, although we weren't ready, we knew that we needed to face what our world was now. Our world without Bo William. The beginning of a life that was going to be without our baby boy. A life that we didn't at all want. But a life that was standing before us. Just waiting. Wayne and I walked up to the front porch steps and collapsed. We sobbed in each other's arms for what felt like hours. We sat on the front stairs and looked at our tree in the front yard. We both watched in amazement as it moved with the wind. We felt the wind upon our cheeks and began to cry again. We pictured Bo's beautiful lips kissing us with every feeling of wind that brushed passed our body. We gathered our strength and courage to enter the house. The house that was once a place that bonded us together, painted dreary and grim now. We opened the door and went inside.

The Day after the Funeral

The day after Bo's funeral, we knew that we needed to get into the clinic to check on the baby in my belly. We called our doctor and tried to explain what happened, she stopped us and said that she already knew. She told us to come in immediately and she would fit us in whenever we got there.

We walked into Dr. Schwogendert's office and, while we were in the waiting room, I was recalling events that had just transpired before we got there. I was sitting in our bathroom getting ready to leave for the baby appointment and I sat on the toilet in tears. I told Wayne that I just wanted to raise my little boy, and Wayne felt the same way. He had so many plans that he made in his mind for him and Bo to complete. For them to hunt together, fish together and spend time outside making memories together. We felt so robbed of being able to raise our little boy. And I felt so guilty for saying that I didn't want any more boys.

The nurse called us into the doctor's office. Dr. Schwogendert cried and apologized for us having to go through something so traumatic. She herself had a 10-month-old baby boy and we always talked about the milestones that our boys were surpassing every time we went in for the pregnancy checkups. Bo was always with me, sitting in his car seat, waiting patiently.

She stood in front of the ultrasound machine, and I couldn't keep my tears in. I cried from the moment we got to the clinic and I just couldn't stop. I heard the baby's heartbeat and I cried some more. Wayne squeezed my hand so tightly when she asked if we wanted to know the sex of the baby. We both looked at each other, not expecting to hear anything about the sex of the baby already, but we both thought that we already knew that the baby was a girl. She pointed to the ultrasound screen and said, "There's the leg, there's the other leg and there's the scrotum."

We gasped in amazement. We couldn't believe it and we cried so hard that we couldn't even speak a word. We just cried and gasped for air. We held onto each other so tightly and cried. Not that we would have been at all disappointed if we would have had a baby girl. No matter what, we were thankful for our baby to be healthy, but we just felt so robbed out of raising our little boy and it seemed so empty without our Bo with us.

Not at all to say that this baby would ever be a replacement. Babies are not meant to do that, just like a parent's love isn't meant to divide, but multiply.

A week later we had our actual ultrasound to confirm the sex of the baby and to make sure that the measurements added up okay. For that appointment, we had to do registration. A lady took my husband and I back into a room and asked us a few questions in regards to insurance and what not. She asked who my primary physician was and I named Dr. Gallagher with confidence. My husband leaned over and said, "No honey, that was Bo's doctor, who delivered him."

Realizing what I said, I was dumbfounded. I couldn't even remember who my own physician was, so I just stared. I could feel my eyes well up with tears. She let us go and sent us upstairs to the ultrasound department. We met the receptionist and I handed her a sheet of paper that was given to me. She then asked what my name was and I just looked at her. I didn't know what was happening or what to do. I heard my husband say, "Amanda

Hartwig, we're here for our 20-week ultrasound." I just shook my head in compliance.

It's like I completely forgot how to communicate and function out in public. It could have also been because the hospital and the clinic were attached. The last time we were near this hospital was on September 4th, the day that Bo died. Looking back now, it was all just too much. My brain was in overdrive trying to protect me. It was essentially in survival mode.

The ultrasound technician took us back and I was already crying a little bit. I told her that she needed to take her time and be extensive in her measurements and to make sure that everything was okay. I explained that just two weeks ago we experienced the death of our 10-month-old baby boy and the amount of stress I was under seemed impossible. She realized who we were and recognized the story. She told us that she had read the obituary in the paper and then she started to cry too. I felt bad for making her cry but I knew that I needed an extensive look to make sure that this baby was okay.

Pregnancy During Child Loss

We were 18 weeks pregnant with our third child when Bo died. There's an undeniable and unshakeable fear when you go through child loss while pregnant. It's a fear that looks you in the mirror every single morning, lingers in the shadows when you're outside, and screams silent echoes when you're inside your still quiet house. We had no choice but to continue with our pregnancy and to keep a sense of hope with our third child.

I'll never forget sitting in the grief counselor's room and getting handed a picture to color to help keep us focused on the present moment. When someone experiences child loss, their mind tends to want to travel back to the past where their child exists, awake and breathing. Or their mind travels to the future where it becomes paralyzing to think about life without their child. When your beloved child dies, the hardest moment to stay in is the present moment. The picture that we colored to keep us in the present moment was called *The River of Life*. There were a lot of different feelings portrayed in the picture—grief and loss, along with all sorts of other "normal" feelings. As soon as Wayne and I were finished coloring the picture, we realized that our son was going to be named, River.

Three weeks after Bo's death, I learned of the term, *Rainbow Baby*. A Rainbow Baby is a baby that is born after the death of an older sibling. Because, very much like a rainbow appearing in the sky after a dark, torrential, turbulent storm, welcoming a new life into your family after the death of your child opens your heart back up to love and allows you to feel the good in your life again. Not as a replacement, but as a promise. As I would soon learn, immense amounts of beautiful after something scary and traumatic is the essence of God's promise.

We would talk about many things in the grief counselor's office, and about half of the time it would be related to River. It was still surreal to me that we were pregnant. Through everything that had happened. Even though I was able to feel his kicks, I felt scared that I wasn't going to develop feelings for him. And at the risk of sounding like a horrible mom, I was incredibly scared that I wasn't going to love River because of the massive amount of grief that was swallowing me up inside from experiencing the death of Bo. I began to wonder if I was going insane.

I started to worry about things that I never thought I would worry about. If the baby is moving, if his heartbeat was strong and current, if his size and length was normal, and just about the general health of the baby. It's a very unfair and undeniable feeling when the grief comes. I was so worried that this baby would die too. I was convinced that I was going to miscarry. I was so sure that lightening would strike again because we had already experienced it. We remember thinking that it would never happen to us. We would hear about children dying and make a little remark but nothing more than that.

I found myself constantly checking my underwear when I was in the bathroom to make sure that I wasn't bleeding. I was sure that it was coming because it felt so hard to think positive when something so devastating and traumatic had already happened. The positive is completely gone. Vanished. Disintegrated. Fear begins to override any ability to think positive thoughts. I tried to keep telling myself that this baby inside me already had a life plan, just like Bo did. And a life is a life on this earth, no matter how brief of time. I started to develop more and more feelings toward River. Although I carried lots of guilt for not wanting to get close to him because I thought he was going to die too.

Normal pregnancies have stress and worry written into the contract already. You know, the unwritten contract that every mother enters into the moment that their pregnancy test confirms a little plus sign or smiley face. I know because of my daughter, Ariana and my son, Bo. Even though I dealt with the death of my grandma, who was my role model, when I was pregnant with Ari, both of my previous pregnancies were considered "normal." That trauma was nothing compared to what we endured with the death of Bo William.

The pregnancy with River was so different. Not even in the same realm of pregnancy, really.

When Bo passed away, I didn't eat anything. I couldn't eat anything. Not a thing. I think that I had a slice of cheese and two bottles of water over the course of the weekend. I didn't eat the day of his funeral, or days afterwards. Eventually, I regained my appetite. The entire pregnancy was a real struggle. I went to the doctor twice a week, sometimes more. Every little scare or feeling that I had was on overdrive. I was hypersensitive to any feeling that felt abnormal to me.

Another difficult situation was the fact that people started to pressure me into being "okay" since I was pregnant and having another baby. They wanted me to start living my life again. That's impossible though. There is a missing part of my heart, and it's shaped exactly like Bo. No one could fill the space, but him. It doesn't just go away. Reality doesn't just change.

In the midst of everything, I would find relief when I journaled, just as I kept a journal for Ariana when she was little, I did the same for Bo:

November 18, 2015:

Good morning sweetheart,

Today I feel extremely grateful. Grateful to you, that I got the amount of time that I did with you and that you chose me to be your mommy.

I feel like the tunnel is lit a little bit more as long as I'm helping someone else and making a difference while I'm here, for you. It may sound strange, but it feels like you're with me when I do it.

I love you beyond any measure. I have hope that you'll continue to be right by my side and continue to guide me so that I'm able to honor you and your memory.

Along with journaling and seeing a grief counselor, I started to see a psychiatrist. I wanted to be completely sure that I was in the right mindset when our rainbow baby arrived. All of this time had passed and I was still overwhelmed with the unbearable amount of guilt that was around me for not being able to give River any sort of attention and love during pregnancy. It felt like a torture chamber for me mentally to be pregnant. I was swallowed whole with grief. Everything I did or said was constantly in question in my mind. But somehow, he thrived through it all.

Therapy

A few days after Bo's funeral, I decided to call Dodge County Human Services to figure out how we would go about finding a therapist. We both admitted that we were having certain thoughts that weren't very productive and we worried for each other. Wayne and I had scary visions right after the funeral happened and we started to get concerned. We just needed reassurance that the thoughts were "normal" given the situation and that we could get through this. When I called Dodge County Human Services, the receptionist answered and was unsympathetic to our situation.

I said, "Hi, my name is Amanda Hartwig. My husband and I just suffered a huge loss in our family and we are in desperate need of help. We are in desperate need of a therapist."

Her response was, "Well, what insurance do you have? Are you aware that you can go through your insurance for therapists *instead* of using our services?"

I was stunned and caught off guard. I wasn't sure what to do so I just hung up the phone.

When I described what happened to my husband, who had been outside at the time, he was shocked that she wasn't more helpful.

About an hour or so passed and I was still so bothered by the way this receptionist handled the situation. She wasn't open to helping us at all. It already felt like we were on our own. Knowing that this was her job, she needed to be more helpful and I was still bothered. I called her back.

After reaching the same woman I said, "My name is Amanda Hartwig, I called before. I need to talk to someone else who is able to help me."

She hesitantly said, "Are you still interested in our services? We can't get you in until October 12th."

I paused for a moment. I was trying so hard not to scream at her because I knew that we desperately needed help.

She continued to babble, as I spoke sternly, "Yes, we are interested in help! That date is NOT going to work for us. What you do not understand is that my son was ten months old; he was not supposed to go this soon! This shouldn't be this way. What I need is more sympathy and understanding from you!"

She didn't say anything, she just paused. I heard the words, "I'm sorry," come through the phone. She explained that she needed to get a hold of her boss to see if she could get us in any sooner.

The woman called back about ten minutes later and said that she got us an appointment for the middle of the following week. The intake worker who did our initial interview is still our therapist to this day. And we love him dearly.

If you are scared to reach out for help, I would caution you to not be your own roadblock. There are so many therapists that have the best intentions, and if you are uncomfortable for any reason, you have the right to change to a different one. The hardest part is to get yourself to go. And as soon as you take that risk, you can allow yourself to start opening up and letting go of all the pent-up anger, anxiety and worries. My husband would always say that we go to therapy because our therapist is our metaphorical garbage can. We would take our "garbage" and lay it all out on the table, and sometimes we would just dump it right over his head. But either way, it got it up and out of our body and mind.

A good therapist will help you understand that whether your

child was in utero, a few years old or 30 years old when they died, they're still your child. Missing your child is okay. Not wanting to be here is okay. They are your baby. And nothing can or will ever take that away! Not even death. If you're seeing a therapist that doesn't make you feel comfortable with telling your story and helping you with your problems, find another therapist. There are thousands out there. And plenty of good ones.

We recommend therapy even if you haven't gone through the death of your child. Because life is hard. In all different directions. In all different seasons. Therapy should be viewed the same as going to the doctor for a routine checkup.

Away with the Hartwigs

The weekend after the funeral was the weekend that we had planned our bed and breakfast honeymoon that a bunch of guests bought us for our wedding present. A "mini honeymoon" for Wayne and me. We had this bed and breakfast planned for months prior to September. We contemplated even going, given our current mindset. We put in some serious thought and decided it might be nice to get away from such a small town where everyone knows you and knows what happened. We couldn't even go into a gas station and not have the workers there stop what they were physically working on just to stare at us. So, we decided to go. We figured if it got too hard on us at any point, we could just drive home. To our surprise we stayed the whole weekend, and we ended up meeting up with some friends that were staying in Wisconsin Dells, about ten minutes away from us. We spent the day walking around, taking a tour on the Dells Duck Boats and going to Ripley's Believe It or Not Museum.

On the drive back to the bed and breakfast, we saw fireworks in the middle of a field. They literally were set off in the middle of nowhere. Wayne told me that he knew that was from our baby Bo. As we got out of the truck and approached the cabin, we looked up and saw what must have been a million stars. The sky was lit up. We both sat down in bed and cried.

We had a good time, but as the night ended, we realized that we did way too much to try to distract ourselves. We felt the familiar heaviness sitting there, lingering and waiting for us.

We spent the remainder of the weekend in misery.

On September 20, 2015, my Aunt Linda called and told me that she knew a spiritual healer and that she wanted to gift us an appointment with her. She already paid her so all we had to do was talk to her.

It was Monday night. Wayne and I drove about an hour to get to her house and we weren't exactly sure what to expect. We said that we were going to keep an open mind and be willing to let anyone or anything help us.

Her name was Rose; she had beautiful white hair and was a bit older. She was beautiful inside and out. She had a calm and gentle sense about her. We walked into her house and we went into a room that was peaceful and immediately relaxing to us.

The reading started and she asked how we've been doing. Usually I would say that's a loaded question but something told me that she already knew how we were doing. We talked about Bo and how happy he was.

Rose looked at Wayne and asked him how he was dealing with this loss. Wayne looked at Rose and said, "I hurt physically."

"Where do you hurt?" she asked.

And just as Wayne muttered about his chest, Rose pointed to his chest too. She told him that he had been worrying so much about other people and their grief over Bo that he wasn't grieving for himself. She told him that he needed to lean in and receive the grief and the process that it needed to take. Rose advised Wayne that if he kept going on this path, he would become very ill due to the added stress of always putting others first. Then she put one hand gently on his chest and the other on his back. He was still sitting in the chair, and she told him to breathe in but when he was about to take a breath he needed to breathe through his back and not so much through his chest. At first Wayne said that he didn't know what she meant, but then he said that he let his guard down and trusted her words. He shut his eyes. I was sitting across from him and I could physically see when he took a breath that the pain left his body. He looked more relaxed with every breath he took after that.

Then Rose sat back down between us. She looked at me and asked the same question.

At first, I honestly didn't know what to say. I thought over and over in my head what I actually felt and there were no actual words. It was emptiness. So that's exactly what I told her.

Rose stopped me in my tracks and said, "No! You need to stay here. I feel you trailing off, I know that you want to be with Bo. But it's not your time right now. You need to stay here. Take those thoughts of leaving out of your mind."

I broke down in tears.

"It just hurts so badly," I muttered.

Rose rubbed my hand and explained that there was no where else for me to be right now, than here on this earth. She helped me to see that Bo would be waiting for me. She explained that I had a mission here, and that I wasn't nearly finished with that mission yet.

A few more minutes went by, and before we left, she gave us a few items to take home.

Wayne and I left feeling some relief and the ability to breathe again. I had been feeling terrible for not being able to tell him my deep thoughts. I wanted to so badly, but I was fearful that it would make him not want to be here either. For that moment, it felt like a load had been lifted off of our shoulders and an elephant was taken out of the room because we were able to honestly communicate with one another.

Rock Bottom

Friday, October 2, 2015 was not a good day for me. It was Hell. I wrote in Bo's journal after everything had happened and this is what it said:

Today is not a good day.
Today was real, real hard, real tough, real Hell.
We're in Hell. I'm in Hell.
It's crazy because when you feel like you can't take anymore hurt and pain, it's as if a freight train hits you and knocks you down harder.
It's as if you're swimming out alone in an ocean and no one is around you.
The waves engulf you; they drown you.
I've never been more thankful for Wayne in my life.
I feel like I'm outcasted by society.
I miss Bo's warmth against me, I miss his wet kisses and I miss him!
I feel like I'm expected to just get up and move on.
I feel like a burden to others who haven't experienced this loss before.
I feel like others look at me like I should just "forget" about my beautiful baby.
Well I can't, and I won't!
Tomorrow is his first birthday party and this was a day that I pictured to be full of love, laughter and smiles.
I know that I'll be a wreck, a real wreck, a grieving wreck.

I tried my hardest to be a good mom and send out the invitations in the mail over a month early.

And here I am.

I'm going to try my hardest to celebrate your life, Bo, with all of our family and friends.

I'm going to try with all of my might to smile when I think of you.

I'm going to try to smile when I talk about you and tell your stories.

Nothing hides the endless fact though that I miss you, Bo, I want you home.

I always want you home.

Wayne was at work and I was doing great until about 8:30AM. I remember getting French toast sticks out to eat for breakfast and waiting until they were done in the microwave. I was watching the numbers as they fell.

5, 4, 3, 2...

The next moment I'm on the floor in the kitchen.

I'm barely breathing from crying so hard and I could feel myself hyperventilating.

I called my husband and I couldn't get any words out through the phone.

He kept telling me to breathe and calm down.

I hung up the phone.

The thought that came into my mind was my son, my son's lifeless body in his crib.

How stiff he was.

His nose dented to the side.

How blue and purple he was. How cold he was.

And just like that, I was back there.

All of a sudden, a feeling of uncontrollable anger came over me. YOU SHOULD HAVE TURNED HIM OVER!

YOU SHOULD HAVE GOTTEN UP IN THE MIDDLE OF THE NIGHT!
YOU COULD HAVE SAVED HIM!
Before I knew it, I was hyperventilating.

I saw Wayne continuing to call me and I couldn't bring myself to answer the phone. I was sobbing uncontrollably and screaming.

I remember saying out loud, "Amanda, you have to hang on. You have to stay here for Ari. You are pregnant. You have to hang on!"

My sweet five-year-old little girl who I pictured devastated at the thought of her mommy dead in the kitchen. I pictured her dealing with another loss and living her life without me. I imagined her graduating, going to college, getting married, all without me. I didn't want to do that to her. I clung to the image of her that I had in my head. Then I fell deeper, further down. I saw Bo and all I wanted was to hold him again. I wanted to feel him against me, and I wanted to hold him. I thought about me being his mother and needing to protect him from all the worries and horrors that I buried deep in my soul. I was supposed to make sure that this didn't happen to my baby boy. But it did.

I texted my husband, "I just can't do this anymore, I'm so sorry."

After I sent it, I realized where my thoughts were headed, I realized where they were going and I begged my mind to slow down. It became a racetrack. It was as if a black shadowed figure was dragging me down a long dark hallway, and my nails were scraping on the floor trying to grab anything to hold onto. Keeping me here in this place.

I was screaming. I felt like the black shadowed person was the devil. And he was having his way with me. I was his playground.

Wayne called again, and I answered with no sound. I was hysterically crying to the point of having no voice. He was on the

other end and was trying to explain that he had called the police and requested a welfare checkup for me because he knew he was too far away and he couldn't get home to me in time.

The cop knocked hard on the front door. I was crying on the ground in our room with photos of Bo surrounding me. I was lying right outside Wayne's closet. Wayne called and I finally answered, he begged me to answer the door for the cop. I peeled myself off of the bedroom floor and saw the police officer that responded to the call on September 4, 2015. I pulled the door open and I couldn't get any words out of my mouth. He asked what was happening and told me to calm down. I was too far past calming down. I fell towards him and he walked me towards a chair.

He sat down next to me, and I tried my hardest to mutter the words, "I miss him so much." The officer was quiet and then said, "I know you do, Amanda." I couldn't calm down, he asked me over and over to take a deep breath. I knew that I needed to calm down because of our other baby that I was carrying inside me. I held my head down and sat forward on the dining room chair. My breathing was shallow and consistent. The pain was so relentless. I couldn't handle it anymore. I was holding on so tightly to a Mickey Mouse that someone had given me in remembrance of Bo.

The chief of police came in and said that he was going to give Wayne a call and let him know what was happening. Just as he left my cell phone went off, the police officer that was sitting next to me answered it. He told Wayne that I was very distraught and that he should consider coming home immediately. He sat back down next to me. I began to form a sentence, with my head still cradled in my hands and Mickey Mouse under my arm in my lap.

I gathered up the courage and said, "There's a gun in here, Todd, and I need you to get it out of this house."

I felt the police officer's demeanor change, immediately.

I rocked back and forth. He paused for a moment and then he asked where it was and I pointed to Wayne's closet door.

The officer opened the closet door and started rummaging through Wayne's shelves as he searched for the handgun. He found the case and the gun in his closet.

All the while, I'm still sitting with my hands holding my head, looking at the floor, watching each tear drop land in the same spot on the ground.

I heard him page the chief of police back into the house, and as he came back in, both of the police officers agreed that he needed to take the gun out of the house. Todd stayed with me. He seemed almost angry because I told him but I knew that I needed to get it out of the house, as a precaution.

"Amanda, answer this honestly, did you think about using that gun?" he asked reluctantly.

I immediately replied, "Yes, I thought about it." I could feel that the whole discussion would change from this point.

He went on to say that if I followed through with those thoughts that I wouldn't get to see Bo anyway because I would be going to Hell instead. I wanted to tell him that I was living in Hell; I was barely surviving this Hell. I just didn't want to hurt anymore and all I wanted to do was be with Bo.

To my surprise though, no one could understand this. Everyone that we told, looked at me like I had "attempted suicide." I didn't attempt anything. I did not open his closet; I did not touch the gun or whatever case it was in. I didn't even honestly know where it was in his closet; all that I knew was that it was there. And that thought, was scary enough for me.

The cop asked me to get some fresh air with him, so I agreed and we sat out on the front step outside the house. He tried so hard to hold a conversation with me, even though I was slightly

reluctant. I just felt so misunderstood that I couldn't get into a deep conversation about anything.

I knew he was just trying to buy time for my husband to get home, and he did a good job trying to distract me, but I just wanted to lay down. I was completely exhausted. I was terrified of my thoughts. He started to tremble and shake because it was so cold outside, I think because I was so distraught, and my blood was so warm, that I didn't even feel the cold.

About five minutes later, I saw Wayne pull up with his work van. The officer explained what had happened inside, and what I had told him about the gun.

Wayne was in agreement with me, he wanted the gun out of the house. He and the officer decided to remove all of the hunting rifles as well just to be safe.

Wayne hugged me and just held on so tightly. He apologized remorsefully for calling the police but I knew and understood why he did. I'm actually thankful that he called them.

The officer decided to leave and told us that if we needed anything else to call him. I explained to Wayne that the invasive thoughts just grew stronger and that was it. He said he understood and just wanted to be safe and make sure that everything was okay. I was thankful that he didn't think that it was an attempt at suicide at all. He got it because he was going through it with me.

The next challenge would be to tell our families that this happened. And we did.

To our surprise, Wayne's parents were very understanding. And they agreed to hold all the guns that the officers removed from our house.

Bo's First Birthday Party

Saturday, October 3, 2015. It was Bo's very first birthday party—and he wasn't there. I had been planning it for months. It was going to be a Mickey Mouse themed party. I bought all of his decorations early. I already had a vision of what I'd be doing to wake him up for the day. I would have snuck into his room and danced around goofy to make him laugh, just so I could hear his sweet little giggle. I pictured him standing in his crib, grabbing the railing, just smiling at me. I pictured singing, "It's your birthday, happy birthday!" Dancing around his room as he would shake his head at how goofy I was in front of him. We would have been silly together.

Immediate family and some friends came over to the house. Only a few of our family members knew that just yesterday, I had the police over at our home. This is when I got very good at hiding my true emotions. This is what I call a grief mask.

We planned to do a balloon release in memory of our sweet Bo. We had written letters to tie to the balloons to send them up to Heaven. In one of my letters I asked his great grandparents in Heaven to read him the letters so he could know what they said. I also wrote, *"I miss you Bo so much and the longing for you never quiets. It never settles. You're on my mind all the time and I hope that you have a fabulous first birthday, a Happy Heavenly Birthday."* I covered the letter in kisses and tears. I can remember trying so hard to hang on, especially for my daughter. Ariana painted Bo a picture of the

two of them. She wanted to send that up with the balloons. The painting was so heavy that the balloons struggled staying afloat. So, we added more of everyone else's balloons to make sure her painting went up to Heaven for him.

Bo's actual birthday fell on Wednesday, October 7, 2015. We wrote in his memory book, *"Mommy and Daddy hope that you have a great birthday up there today. We miss you more than all the words that this world could ever describe and we love you to infinity and beyond. We hope that you'll be celebrating with all the other little Mouseketeers and will be saying, 'Oh toodles!' Please be around us today. Your sissy, mommy and daddy love when you make your presence known. We are going to light another candle today for you to blow out. We love you sweetheart and wish you were here right now!"*

Our Rainbow

We were so thankful on February 1, 2016, when we welcomed our littlest bear, River William Hartwig, to the world. God had delivered us our rainbow. His promise.

Dr. Schwogendert thought that it would be best for us to set up an induction date, so we went in a week early. The night before, Wayne and I stopped at Walgreens for last minute essentials. We just took a few extra strolls around the isles to talk. It was the last moments that we would be a family of four. And we knew it.

I spent weeks writing up a birth plan and rules for seeing our new baby. I became an overly obsessed mom who was hellbent on keeping her child safe. I felt like I was entering motherhood for the first time all over again. Where moms that are on their third child usually have all of the stuff down and can consider themselves experts in the parenting area, I felt like I had lost all of my confidence with the death of Bo.

The birth plan consisted of the rules for River after he was born. I wanted him on me immediately, and to start skin to skin contact. I wanted Wayne to cut the cord and to deliver him. But most importantly, when the nurses on each shift came in to check on River, I wanted them to be sure that they knew that we were parents of child loss. We didn't want to have to answer any types of questions about our other kids right then. We just wanted to focus on River. I had typed and printed out rules for seeing River that consisted of sanitizing all the time, wearing face masks, not to come around if anyone had a cough or cold and to not, under any circumstances, kiss our baby. Everyone was very understanding.

They started the medicine for induction, and I tried everything to make it move faster. Wayne and I sat in the whirlpool together. I was so thankful that we got that time together. He was able to hold me while I leaned my back up against him. As we watched the time slowly pass by, we both kept hoping that River would come at 10:07AM because that would match Bo's birthday, but Riv had other plans.

The doctor said that he wouldn't touch six pounds at birth, given all of the trauma that my body endured throughout the pregnancy, with the substantial loss of appetite and weight loss. So, we packed premature clothes for River, and expected him to be in the hospital a little bit longer than normal.

When it was finally time to deliver River, the doctor helped guide Wayne's hands and before I knew it, Wayne set him gently on my chest.

I panicked and I kept yelling, "He's not breathing!"

As I watched everyone else clean up from the birth, I felt like no one was helping me. For a couple seconds, I was alone and felt like I was about to relive my nightmare again.

Finally, Wayne touched my shoulder and said, "He's okay, sweetheart, he's breathing just fine."

As I sobbed over River, and the fact that he was here, Wayne said, "He looks a lot bigger than six pounds."

Just as he said that one of the nurses was wheeling the scale in. River weighed in at a whopping ten pounds, seven ounces! We took that as a sign of Bo being with us because Bo's birthday was October 7th (10/7).

The different amounts of hormones and grief I was experiencing was a whirlwind that I wasn't sure how to maneuver. But after the nurses took his vitals, we were left to have a little peace and bonding time. Wayne and I both did skin to skin and after about an hour with us together bonding with River, we decided to let our family in to see him.

It was a sigh of relief when Ariana saw him for the first time. I could tell that she was a little scared because of all that she had endured. But she held him and snuggled him just like she did with Bo. It was beautiful.

Days after we brought River home, I made an appointment to see my psychiatrist. He was pretty confident that I would suffer from postpartum depression since it was evident with my first two children. The only issue would be that the emotions would be very difficult to decipher from grief and postpartum hormones. They prescribed me a medication to help, but it wasn't the same medication that I had after I had Bo. This medication made me emotionally vulnerable in every situation. I would cry all day long. Inevitably, it put a strain on our marriage.

Whether it was the medication, or the paralyzing fear, I still struggled to bond with River. I was convinced that since he didn't die in my womb, he was going to die outside of it. I made up scenarios in my mind of waking up and having to perform CPR on his tiny body too. With the invasive thoughts that I was still continuing to have, it was decided mutually between the psychiatrist and myself that we switch to a different medication.

I continued to voice my struggles to make sure that I wasn't internalizing them. I would see my psychiatrist and therapist regularly. I would make doctor appointments to make sure that River was growing okay and that he seemed healthy, even though I struggled to trust the doctor's opinion because Bo was a healthy baby.

I continued to breastfeed River, to the point that I developed the obsessive-compulsive idea that if I stopped breastfeeding him, he would surely die. I met with breastfeeding coaches and other professionals that would be able to help me ensure the success of our breastfeeding journey. I became addicted to taking gloves from the doctor's office, masks to have around the house in case anyone become sick and I took stock in hand sanitizer. Thankfully, everyone was very accommodating.

It was at this point that I learned that my breastmilk had tiny antibodies in them that would fight off any type of cold or sickness that River had. I was told at one point to put my breastmilk under a microscope and watch all of the little organisms move. Those organisms worked to protect and grow my little one. I breastfed River until he was almost three years old. He was completely dependent on me to be his primary source of nutrition. This was also where my depression and anxiety skyrocketed. River wanted to be breastfed all the time at a specific place on the couch. It had to be my right boob, not my left. I was forced to have my feet reclined, and his head positioned just right. Before I knew it, the housework fell to the wayside, and all I turned into was a walking baby comforter. River summoned me for everything. If he was hurt, tired, ill, cranky, sad, happy and so much more. I had to be in that same spot, with my boob completely out and uncovered.

I won't deny that, although I was extremely depressed because of the wear and tear breastfeeding had on my entire body, and the stress of sitting in one place at his beck and call, this is also the point that allowed our relationship to grow and transform into something beautiful.

Hell and The Clubhouse

We were pregnant and driving to the next county over to grief counseling sessions and child loss support groups when I realized that we needed to do something in Dodge County. It was an idea that was thrown around and then eventually became an idea that we pursued. God put it on my heart to start an organization that would help local families.

I did extensive research on how to start and successfully run a charity organization, and then how to make it a certified charity organization.

The whole process took about six months. And then we decided to make our "birth" of our charity the same month that Bo left this earth. I couldn't think of a better way to honor him.

In September of 2016, after Bo's one-year angelversary, we hosted the *1ˢᵗ Annual Bo William Hartwig Memorial Ride and Fundraiser*. With those funds, we were able to fill out, what felt like, endless forms with the IRS and to pay the fees that that process incurred. We utilized additional funds to cover the cost of other non-profit start up requirements.

And then, Wayne and I decided to launch Bo's Heavenly Clubhouse, A 501(c)(3) certified nonprofit charity organization that is dedicated to helping parents that are suffering with the death of their beloved child. We provide many different avenues of support. And with the help of amazing board members and volunteers, Bo's Heavenly Clubhouse still currently runs and is accessible to families of child loss today. We have helped hundreds of families gain hope and healing. And we hope to help hundreds of thousands more.

Bo's Heavenly Clubhouse was born on the foundation to never give up hope because feeling hopeless is something that is on the forefront of everyone's ability when walking through the trenches of child death. On the days that a parent confides in us, we spend our time trying to make sure that we breathe hope into their lives again. Somehow. However long it takes for hope to reignite, that's how long we wait. This means that we are always open and always available. At the beck and call of any parent that needs us.

We send out care packages nationwide to families that are suffering with the death of their child.

The care packages often consist of a Holy Bible, various child loss books such as *Mother of All Mothers* written by Angela Miller, and *Suffer Well* written by Dan Herod. We also add coloring books and colored pencils, which may sound completely crazy, but focusing on coloring can actually help someone suffering a difficult loss stay focused on the present. Our goal is to help them stay in the present moment by giving them positive grieving tools to put in their grieving toolbox.

We help parents handle the financial burden of funeral costs for their child.

In the days after the loss of a child, all parents should have to worry about is saying goodbye. They should focus on those last moments of breathing their child in, and memorizing every little detail of their precious face. We want them to count their fingers and toes, and then count them again. We want them to get their child dressed for the last time, and comb their hair once more. Often times the parents don't know that we send the funeral directors a check, and we don't need them to. We understand how impeccable the last moments of life are. Before they have no more time with them, like an hour glass that has run out of sand, and all they have are memories to hold and look back on. We want them to take in every last waking detail in.

We also host Child Loss Support Groups the second and fourth Monday of every month.

With each support group that we have hosted, the more and more these once strangers, become family. It's a really nerve-racking feeling when parents come to the support group for the first time. We stress to each new member that it doesn't matter if the members come one time or if they return 20 times. Each time they come to group our goal is to make sure they're as comfortable as possible. We encourage members to come, even if they don't want to speak, they don't have to. We have had parents attend that cry the whole time and don't say a word, and we have also had parents attend and talk a lot. We laugh together. We cry together. It all depends on what the feeling is that night. The one consistent thing that we say in every loss group is that everything that is discussed stays within those four walls. The most important detail is that we are together, and we are not alone.

We also help by making memorial pieces, like marble plaques, with children's photos on them and "Bo Lions" which are stuffed animals constructed of children's clothing. We also send grief care packages nationwide, and provide financial help with final expenses such as funeral costs for children that are 18 years and younger.

Running a charity organization wasn't at all what I had in mind, it wasn't even on my radar of life, but just like that, we were thrown into our new lives. And before I knew it, the healing started to come. We developed deep relationships with parents that attended our support groups. We signed on an amazing set of dedicated volunteer board members that made the internal workings of Bo's Heavenly Clubhouse run smoothly. But Wayne and I were still very early into our grief. And that grief demanded to be felt.

Even years later, the time capsule of child death still has its grip on us. And if we're being honest, I don't foresee that grip ever changing. Years fly by, and it still feels like yesterday that Bo was here. It was 1,493 days ago that Bo died. And I still think of him EVERY single day. I can tell you that it sure doesn't feel like it has been over one thousand days without my sweet boy. It feels like just yesterday that he was here. This is why I refer to grief as a time capsule because even though days pass by, your mind still remembers the important memories that it needs to in order to remember your child. And when those memories are all that remains, they become somewhat of a lifeline. Something that gets replayed consistently throughout the day when the tears and pain are too overwhelming.

Imagine, your child that is no longer physically on this earth. Imagine the number of tears that are spent mourning for that child, and pining over their scent, their voice, and their warmth. A child that was loved so deeply. Gone.

But yet people that haven't experienced the death of their child, or people who don't have children are so quick to tell us bereaved to GET OVER IT. Move on. The list goes on and on.

It's almost as if a limb or another body part is permanently missing and still needing to go on with life. It doesn't work like that. Getting over something of this magnitude shouldn't even be a sentence that comes out of anyone's mouth. Child death is so painful, whether that death is prolonged, drawn out or sudden, it still demolishes the human heart from the inside out.

How could something so heartless be something that some people are so quick to say? It happens quite often, more than one could believe. Many parents come to us in tears because a person that they thought they could trust and depend on throughout this grief process has up and abandoned them. Sometimes it's too great of a burden to bear for some friends and sometimes even family members. But this is where Bo's Heavenly Clubhouse comes in.

We convince parents that are heartbroken and devastated by the death of their beloved child, that grief brings out the best or the worst in people. And if people show their true colors during such a life changing period of time, listen to them. Not their advice. Don't bother listening to their heartless, ignorant advice. Listen to their words. If their words crush your soul and spirit when they should uplift and compassionately care for you, then let them go.

Although we faced death in the eye, every single day, God made a magnificent way for us to help others. And it's through helping other parents and families that were suffering with the death of their child, that we found our true calling. We found true healing.

That's not to say that we didn't have any hardships along the way. Sometimes I would have to face things that I had not ever even considered before, things that would shake me to my very core.

July 7, 2017, I transitioned from writing in my journal to writing on a blog that was for Bo's Heavenly Clubhouse. I knew that I needed an outlet for what I had just experienced:

An emotional day came upon me yesterday. As I was called by a fellow loss mom who had previously endured two miscarriages.

In all of the months leading up to this point, my go to sourcing quote was "Have Faith – Have Faith because God's got this!" Even when I didn't have a strong faith myself, I knew there was a bigger plan. Bigger than what my brain had the capacity to fathom. Bigger than our biggest fear. Deeper than our deepest secret. God has a storyline for us.

But then it happened. She called. Baby Noah was delivered.

All I kept praying was, "Dear God, let her say that he is okay!" I began to get restless with nerves.

"No heartbeat. How can this be?" she began questioning.

"He was just here. Hours ago, he was kicking me, Amanda. How can this be?" she sobbed.

I could feel the lump crawl up my throat, all I could say was, "I'm on my way!"

Driving to the hospital was one of the longest silent drives but walking the hallways to find the hospital room that they were in was even longer.

And as I turned the corner to their hallway, I felt all the anticipation in my chest for what was to come.

I came upon the room; the door was open. And there he was. There she was. Mom. Defeated. Holding her sweet baby boy. My heart sank. I felt completely depleted.

All of the days that she would call me in complete panic, and all of the times that I would be on the other line of the phone telling her that it would be okay came rushing back at once.

I tiptoed in; I felt the tears well up in my eyes. This beautiful mother had delivered her baby. Her baby born sleeping.

This same strong mother was told "there was no heartbeat" just hours prior, now holding her precious baby that she had delivered to this world, knowing the daunting, unchangeable outcome. I sat down beside her; I couldn't do anything but stare at her, and hold her. I held both of them. I tried to muster up any form of a sentence but the lump in my throat was so big.

Sitting beside her, rubbing her back, I watched her heartbreak, her brokenness and defeat. I witnessed her complete devastation. I carefully took in the entirety of the moment. Her soft caresses to his bottom. Cradling him, him swaying so perfectly in her arms. Knowing that this would be the first, last and only time

that she would get to hold her beloved child in her arms.

Then she asked it. A question that I was not at all prepared for. One that I didn't even think about prior to leaving the house.

"Do you want to hold him?" she quietly asked.

It took me but a moment, a moment to think about my babies. My beloved children that I've held so carefully in my arms. And as I took baby Noah in my arms, I saw each one of my children. I saw Ari, my firstborn and I was beyond scared. I saw Bo, my first little boy. My sweet boy. And I saw River, who was my rainbow after my torrential storm. All of our children are miracles, just like little Noah.

And so, I held him. I studied his face.

As I sat there for a moment, I felt myself outside of my body. Almost as if I were a balloon filled with helium. A balloon that was just floating off. Floating off to the place that I do not like to go. That place that welcomes me every time I enter it. The one place that torments me. That place where the devil lives, lingers and prods at me when I'm feeling weak.

My balloon wandered for but a moment. And in that moment, I was walking through his bedroom door. Grabbing him up and doing compressions. I was shrieking with all my might. Pressed up against his tiny lips, his against mine, blowing everything I had into him. Praying that it would be enough. Just enough to make him wake up. Praying that it would be enough to save him. Praying that this would all be a nightmare that I could overcome.

I was in the Beaver Dam Hospital. Watching the doctor do those same compressions. Watching his body move with each push on his little body. Seeing Bo hooked up to an EKG and feeling his ice-cold body. Broken. Lying next to him, whispering.

"Please baby, Mommy is here. Let's get up and go home. Please, Bo."

NO. I DID EVERYTHING THAT I COULD. GET THESE THOUGHTS AWAY FROM ME!

I felt my mind become a battlefield. It's not about me! It's about Noah! Stop it!...I struggled.

But as I regained control of my balloon, I came back down to the present moment. I was back at the hospital. I was back with Noah. I was back in my life right now, my life without Bo.

As I witnessed this mother's strength and love for her son, I was reminded that he didn't hurt. He never felt pain. He didn't have to endure surgery or broken bones. He was loved his entire life, and felt nothing but warmth from his mother. As I gave Noah back to his mom, I realized a beautiful fact.

How beautiful is it to think that the very first thing he saw when his little eyes opened was the face of Jesus? The face of Jesus. Our Creator. Our God.

That my friend, is all the fight you should ever need. To this mother, you know who you are, you are an inspiration to so many. Please don't give up, keep going in your child's memory. Keep talking about your children. Your babies love you and continue loving you from afar.

Still managing to tend to other hurting hearts drove something deep inside my heart. I held babies that were born sleeping, attended numerous funerals for children that looked like sleeping angels, sent out hundreds of care packages, planning fundraisers, and so much more. It began to give me a sense of purpose. Meanwhile, I was still sifting through my own grief, trauma and healing. It became very much a two-way street. At this time, I was also having terrible nightmares. I won't ever be able to forget my most morbid one...*I found myself at the cemetery where Bo's spot was.*

I found a shovel and started to dig.

Suddenly the casket was in an old hospital.

I opened the casket and there he was.

He looked perfect. Sleeping.

And then he wasn't. He started to move.

In the most sinister way. He began to twitch his limbs.

And then he sat up. He wasn't able to hold his head up though. It wobbled.

At this time a county sheriff busted through the double doors with his gun drawn.

He wasn't pointing it at me. though. He was pointing it at Bo.

The sheriff yelled out to him,

"WHO ARE YOU?"

As he wobbled around, his foot fell from the table.

A deep voice came out of his mouth, from what sounded like the pits of Hell.

"I AM LUCIFER!"

Demonic and sinister.

I woke up.

Cold Sweats. Screaming. Crying hysterically.

Grabbing onto Wayne as if I was drowning.

Trying to explain to him what I saw.

But I couldn't because I didn't want him to see our son like that.

I didn't want to see our son like that!

And this right here. This is what I call, HELL.

It can't possibly be described any other way. The devil had a foothold in our home, in my life, in my dreams. And these dreams were the worst of my nightmares. I woke up completely frozen, full of sweat and tears. Paralyzed by what I saw and what I felt. I felt the attack on my heart now more than ever before.

Days passed and I was still struggling with the gruesome nightmare that I endured. The secretary of the board and I had

become very close because we were both stay at home moms. I was so scared to talk about my nightmares because I didn't want to give them any attention, but they were weighing on my soul. So, out of desperation, I told Jessica and I could feel how serious the dream was by her response, "Have you prayed about it?" she asked.

I was shocked that this was her response. I had just finished telling her about my terrible nightmare and she asked if I had prayed about it?

"Well…" I started, but what could I say? I had not prayed about it. What would praying do? What on earth would that change?

I'll be the first one to admit that, before Bo died, we didn't attend church on a regular basis. We went to a Catholic Church every once in a while, particularly on holidays. When we attended this church, we were never taught how to pray or what to even say. We just simply replied with whatever the speaker told us to say. There was no real thought process involved. So even though we went to church, we didn't pray. We weren't utilizing the full power of God. We didn't have a relationship with our Creator.

And suddenly, as I sat there with Jessica, I felt a brisk chill crawl up my spine. Prayer. I could pray. And I began to contemplate. What could it hurt? I was desperate enough to try because there had to be more than these morbid nightmares. There had to be a way to control these invasive thoughts. There had to be more than this excruciating pain.

Later that afternoon, I was home alone and I couldn't fight the urge to do some research. How do people pray? How do I pray? What are the basic concepts of prayer? These sounded like great questions for Google.

Heaven

I came across the *Bible App* that was available for my phone. To make it that much more convenient to learn about Jesus. I downloaded it and started to research scripture after scripture. And before I knew it, there was a hunger that was awakened in my heart. I had many different questions that I previously thought I had the answers to. Now, after reading through scripture, I realized that I had finally found the true answers.

I realized that the healing that I was searching for, everything that we have endured after Bo's death, was wrong. We were looking in the wrong places. We were leaning on the wrong things to help our hearts. Spiritual healers. Mediums. We were trying to mend the pain with things that could never fulfil the power of peace. We were putting our hope into things that weren't designed with the ability to give us peace.

So, I prayed, my very first *real* prayer, ever:

"God, I really don't know what I'm doing. Or if you're really there. I have been having horrible dreams and I don't really know what else to do. I'm scared and I don't want to picture Bo like this. I need your help, okay?"

I asked as if He would answer back in an audible voice.

(However, now I know that from time to time, if you quiet your mind enough, He does audibly answer.)

But I felt so silly praying for the first time. I felt silly praying for the first thirty times, to be completely honest! Eventually, it got easier. And I got softer. The anger that was originally pointed at God, morphed into a true, desperate need for Him.

I began to feel a peace in my heart. Peace that I have NEVER experienced before. A peace that is completely indescribable with human words. And the terrible nightmares that I was enduring had dissipated. Before I knew it, I became a believer. God started a work in me, and awoke a hunger for Jesus.

I can still recall enduring those terrible thoughts, and those unrelenting invading images that would just pop into my mind. Unsolicited. Unwelcome.

But rehearsing a verse from the Bible, aloud, sometimes ten, or twenty times if I had to, helped me tremendously:

"Away from me, Satan!" Which is what Jesus said as Satan was tempting him while he was in the desert and fasting for forty days.

Matthew 4:1-11 – Then Jesus was led by the Spirit into the wilderness to be tempted by the devil. After fasting forty days and forty nights, he was hungry. The tempter came to him and said, "If you are the Son of God, tell these stones to become bread." Jesus answered, *"It is written: 'Man shall not live on bread alone, but on every word that comes from the mouth of God.'"* Then the devil took him to the holy city and had him stand on the highest point of the temple. "If you are the Son of God," he said, "throw yourself down. For it is written: He will command his angels concerning you, and they will lift you up in their hands, so that you will not strike your foot against a stone.'" Jesus answered him, *"It is also written: 'Do not put the Lord your God to the test.'"* Again, the devil took him to a very high mountain and showed him all the kingdoms of the world and their splendor. "All this I will give you," he said, "if you will bow down and worship me." Jesus said to him, *"Away from me, Satan! For it is written: 'Worship the Lord your God and serve him only.'"* The devil left him, and angels came and attended him.

And each time that I would say this aloud, to fight the unwarranted thoughts that would completely debilitate me, I was able to combat the horror.

I would often use "Away from me, Satan" and on the days that I needed something differently, I would pull out the verses from Matthew 16:22-23, when Jesus is explaining to His disciples what must take place in the upcoming hours.

Matthew 16:22-23 – Peter took him aside and began to rebuke him. "Never, Lord!" he said. "This shall never happen to you!" Jesus turned and said to Peter, *"Get behind me, Satan! You are a stumbling block to me; you do not have in mind the concerns of God, but merely human concerns."*

Mark 8:31-33 – He then began to teach them that the Son of Man must suffer many things and be rejected by the elders, the chief priests and the teachers of the law, and that he must be killed and after three days rise again. He spoke plainly about this, and Peter took him aside and began to rebuke him. But when Jesus turned and looked at his disciples, he rebuked Peter. *"Get behind me, Satan!"* he said. *"You do not have in mind the concerns of God, but merely human concerns."*

I was able to picture whatever terrible thought I was having, and turn it into a million little pieces of soot and ash behind me. Then I would witness the pieces fall to the ground. The manner of authority in which Jesus spoke, gave me such confidence knowing that authority and power was accessible to me.

Maybe it was the thirtieth time, or maybe the one hundredth, but all at once there was a time when I walked right up to the feet of Jesus, and I laid those guilty feelings down in front of Him. Instead of the horror slithering its way into my mind, I could build a wall to keep them out. Just like that, I had power.

That's not to say that I didn't pick those feelings up again, the next day, or the next. Somedays, I would refuse to let the feelings go, I would wallow in the fact that I could have saved my beloved son, if I would have known what was coming. The sad truth is, that battle may not ever be over. Whether I completely leave it at the feet of Jesus or not, but the important concept was that I was able to recognize the rabbit hole and acknowledge the fact that I didn't have to travel down it anymore.

I could stop the words that would creep in, so uninvited. The thoughts of needing and wanting to do more. More to save my beloved son. The thoughts of what I should have done instead. The thoughts of what I could have done. The thoughts of what I would have done if I knew that he was sick. I would lay the lies from Hell down at Jesus' feet and I would try with all my might to not pick them up again.

If this is where you are right now, as you're reading this, I am so sorry. I don't know your situation or the way your child died. But I do know that common ache, the agonizing desire for your child to be back in your arms.

The "should have, could have, would have" thoughts are dangerous. They are an endless pit of horror. Because it will leave you alone, depressed, restless, and void of all hope.

I have probably gone over a thousand different ways that I would have saved Bo. And if I'm not careful, I mean extremely careful, those thoughts can quickly morph into a false depiction of the kind of mother I view myself as. I know in my heart that I'm a *good* mom. Because I *am* in agony. I wouldn't be in this agony if I didn't love Bo so much. Which is what makes me a good mommy. And what a bittersweet feeling to not want the worst pain of your life to stop hurting, because it reminds you of how much you still *love* your child. The pain reminds you of how deep that love is.

If only someone would have warned me not to go down the

paths of wishing I could have done something differently. The endless tunnel of could haves, should haves and would haves.

But it is *so* easy to go down that road, the one where you paint a different outcome in your mind. The constant truth that I always tried to reign in was that I did all that I could. I hated being told that I did everything I could.

In November 2015, Bo's coroner received the results of his autopsy and called and asked to come over. He got down on his knees in our living room, looked us in the eyes, and told us that we did everything that we could have done. A pill so difficult to swallow at such a crucial moment in our lives. We were told that we did all we could do. How could this be? We're his parents. We should have done more. Something more. The results of his autopsy were in. Bo died of the Adenovirus, which is the common cold.

According to Google Dictionary, the Adenovirus is any of a group of DNA viruses first discovered in adenoid tissue, most of which cause respiratory diseases.

But how could this be? Our baby had a slight fever and then the fever broke. He went to bed smiling!

Bo's coroner went on to explain that even if we did take him to the hospital, there would have been a million to one chance that the doctors would have tested for something like this in his system.

We were devastated. The odds were stacked up against us.

It was a huge transformation when we realized that we were not in control of what happened. We couldn't help him, even if we would have done something more.

This outlook reigns true for many scenarios. Not just some. Drug addiction, suicide, whether your child died slowly, or they left so abruptly that your heart didn't get a chance to say goodbye. It was out of your control.

You have to believe that if you had the chance to change the outcome, we both know that you would have. *I know that you would have.*

THIS is what makes you a GREAT parent.

The fact that you want and pine so deeply in the middle of your own agony to make a different outcome for your child.

The fact that most of us parents, would lay our lives down for our child in a heartbeat. I know I would have.

Our brains are built to problem solve. So, it is to be expected that when we face trauma, like the death of our child, our brains will replay this horror movie over and over and over again. Similar to a broken film or a movie that is stuck on repeat. Our brains will actually continue to try to "solve the problem," even when the problem is deemed unsolvable. Our brains don't know any differently.

That's why our brains will come up with millions of different ideas, and ways that it could have been different. Ways that would give a different outcome and solve the problem.

But when you realize that this is how our brains are wired, you are then able to understand why these thoughts come. This is why saying something aloud like, "Get behind me Satan!" or "STOP!" will wake your brain up and allow you to move on to the next thought. I've had to do this process hundreds of times. Before I started to realize how important it truly was to wake my brain up instead of traveling down the rabbit hole that is so dark and draining.

Then, the importance is *shifting* your focus. Not *forgetting.* Or *ignoring.* But rather, shifting your focus to something else for a minute. The point of being grounded into the present moment. For me, it was Bible reading. I started to learn more and more; I learned the importance of Baptism. And dedicating your life to God.

I decided to read about the importance of being baptized after you become a believer. After you decide to dedicate your life to Christ, after you say to Him, "I am a child of God." After you understand the importance of following Him and the true freedom He is able to give you access to.

All throughout scripture, baptism happens only after you become a believer. This is because we are meant to *die* to our flesh and sins. It is so important to recognize the sins and repent of them. Repenting means asking for forgiveness.

Sin is so sneaky. It enables us to believe that nothing is wrong and it captures us in its snare and keeps us in bondage. It doesn't matter what the sin is that you've committed, it will eat you alive.

It will take any sort of peace that you have left, and devour it. The devil will convince you that you're not worthy of repentance. Satan will try to convince you that you're not worthy of salvation. And that is a lie from Hell.

But we also need to recognize that sin is very difficult to recognize if we don't want to acknowledge it. Baptism is a symbolic representation of taking those dirty rags of sin and making them clean. We are those rags.

Ephesians 4:5 – One Lord, One Faith, One Baptism.

You are responsible for your own salvation. If you've had your children baptized, that's great. Bo was baptized. Actually, all of our children were. But that was before we became "awoke."

Children are all welcome in God's Kingdom.

Until you get to an age where you are able to understand and can choose with your own free will, all of the children of God go directly to Him.

They're HIS.

And that is a truly wonderful thought.

*Matthew 19:14 – Jesus said, **"Let the little children come to me, and do not hinder them, for the kingdom of heaven belongs to such as these."***

So, I was able to gain peace by seeing and reading these scriptures, I started to talk to other parents that have endured the death of their child. And once I started to get to know some of the other parents of child loss, it gave me a weird sense of hope. A hope that I wasn't alone. And that I didn't have to endure this excruciating pain alone.

It gave me a hope in knowing that if they could get through this, we could get through this too.

It's so hard to believe that when your child dies, the world still continues to turn. Life continues to happen. Most people expect you to continue on where you left off in life. Even though you're missing a piece of your heart. Even though for you, the world has come to a complete stop. Even though, for you, the world has turned upside down.

I felt an unexplained amount of peace being around other parents of child loss and understanding that whether we liked it or not, we shared a special bond that not a lot of people would be able to understand. And while we found peace in being with other parents of child loss, we were also finding peace with knowing that Bo is okay. He is HOME. Where we all are desiring to go. I believe that Bo had a very special mission here. A mission that was designed by God, and when he fulfilled that mission, Bo went home.

And the true beauty is, the relationship isn't severed. Death cannot kill love. Death does not negate existence. His love is still there for me, just as I know that he still feels mine.

Whether you've experienced miscarriage, or if you've delivered your baby born sleeping.

Whether you brought your baby home and they couldn't stay, or your "baby" made it to adolescent years.

Maybe your child made it to adulthood.

God says that He knitted us while we were in our mother's womb.

That means, sweet mama, I'm talking to you—your sweet child is known and loved.

They are known and loved by the One who created the moon, the sun and the stars.

The Creator of the universe.

He loves you.

He LOVES your children.

And what a beautiful gift He has entrusted you with.

To love these children that are really, *His.*

Psalm 139:13 – For you created my inmost being; you knit me together in my mother's womb.

I began to dwell and find comfort in the idea that God knew Bo *already.* And this delivered such relief to my heart. I had victory over the enemy when I had this revelation. I was no longer a playground for Lucifer. He was no longer welcome in my heart. He was no longer welcome in my home. He was no longer welcome around my family.

But one of Satan's sly moves is to make you doubt yourself. He will make you doubt your ability in parenting, decision-making and any other ability that you have in your life. Satan prides himself on being able to persuade you in misery. He wants you to believe that this entire agony is God's fault. And that you don't need Jesus in your life. Satan wants you to believe that you deserve this. Something he almost got me to believe was that I wasn't able to get through this. He wanted me to believe that there is no power in numbers. He almost had me believing that I was meant to be alone.

But these are all lies. More lies from Hell.

We were not designed to be alone. So, when we endure agony and hardship, our souls are actually meant to collaborate with each other. To breathe hope into each other. To breathe life and love into each other's lives. It's what we're all called to do. We're called to intercede in prayer for each other, when someone doesn't feel strong enough to pray for themselves.

Even though I didn't *know* God, HE had been there this WHOLE TIME. Even though I didn't have a relationship with Jesus, it didn't matter. He knew Bo. And He *loves* Bo. He *loves* me. He *loves* you.

Because essentially, we all come from God. He knows all of us and the plan for our life is written in His book. Even if we don't have a relationship with Him.

Our children are only gifts that He entrusts to us. He entrusts them with us. It is our job to grow them up in God and to teach them the ways of Jesus. We need to be teaching them how to fight their spiritual battles because they will have some of their own someday.

Proverbs 22: 6 – Train up a child in the way he should go: and when he is old, he will not depart from it.

He deeply desires a relationship with us as soon as we can comprehend it. You can see this all throughout scripture in the Old and New Testament.

So, I figured out that God wanted a relationship with me. But I wasn't sure how to attain it. After all, what is so special about me? The answer is that He has always desired a relationship with me. He has always desired a relationship with you, too!

We are made in His image (Genesis 5:3).

And it was here that I discovered my importance. And it is here that you can discover yours.

After countless days of praying, I began to feel my faith get stronger. Brick by brick, I began building a relationship with my creator. I started opening my heart to God. I started talking to Him every day, at all times of the day.

It was an act that started out of complete desperation, I wanted to believe that there had to be more to this world than this pain. The agony that I was in was completely paralyzing.

And then we were invited to an Apostolic Pentecostal Church, which was unlike ANYTHING that we had ever experienced. Their prime foundation of beliefs is based off of Acts 2:38.

Peter replied, "Repent and be baptized, every one of you, in the name of Jesus Christ for the forgiveness of your sins. And you will receive the gift of the Holy Ghost."

Our family started to attend Cornerstone UPC Church on a semi regular basis, with slight apprehension from Wayne. It took him a long time to be honest about his feelings toward the church. I was all in with nothing to lose, but Wayne couldn't get there. He was stuck on how different this church was from anything else that he had ever experienced before.

The feeling that I took home after church each time we would go would be unreal. I felt like I had learned something each time I would go, and I discovered a real hunger for more. I received the Holy Ghost and spoke in other tongues on July 10, 2016. I felt overwhelmed with joy and so many other emotions. I did not understand what I said as my tongue surrendered to Jesus. I felt His presence flow into my heart as if I was swallowing a warm cup of tea and it made its way into the pits of my soul. It is biblical that we are to surrender and tame our tongue, the most powerful muscle in our entire body.

Proverbs 21:23 – Whoever keeps his mouth and his tongue keeps himself out of trouble.

Proverbs 12:18 – The words of the reckless pierce like swords, but the tongue of the wise brings healing.

A biblical concept that is all throughout the Bible. It sounds a little crazy, and different, if you have never experienced the gift of speaking in other tongues. But once we invite Jesus into our lives and allow His spirit to flow through us, we gain access to this spiritual language. This is accessible to you and anyone that you know. The gift of speaking in other tongues is an additional way that we are allowed to access the Holy Spirit. If we surrender all pride, and set aside the worry of our flesh of feeling or looking silly or dumb, we give Him all the power that He deserves. He claims victory over our bodies, our souls, our lips and our tongues.

1 Corinthians 14:39 – Therefore, my brothers and sisters, be eager to prophesy, and do not forbid speaking in tongues.

Days and months passed us by, and things seemed like they were falling back into place. I was able to reclaim a little bit more of my joy back.

Until they weren't falling into place at all.

Things were incredibly difficult once I decided to take our family consistently to an Apostolic Pentecostal church.

One day after, what I thought, was an amazing sermon at Cornerstone UPC Church, I leaned into Wayne and said, "Baby, for the first time since Bo died, I feel hope and joy. This church is exactly what we needed."

He looked back at me sharply, "Maybe it's what YOU needed, we've never done church that way, and I was kind of uncomfortable. I would like to go back to the Catholic church that we started with, next to where Bo is buried."

I was totally shocked. And I felt my heart sink once again in my stomach.

As days brushed by, our marital pages only seemed farther and farther apart. Until they were in separate books entirely. I would cry out to him about his lack of interest in Cornerstone UPC and

I would beg him to reconsider where he would be going to church. I would beg him to take the place as head of household spiritually and start to pray with and for us. The worse things got at home, the more my heart desired to be at Cornerstone church. I felt such a release when I would allow myself to let all of my anger towards my husband out to God. I would cry and sob on my knees at the altar. Every Sunday and Wednesday.

I decided that, in addition to Sunday mornings, the children and I would also go on Wednesday nights. But Wayne absolutely refused. Some Wednesdays he would request that the kids stay home with him, so I would carpool with a few friends. I would cry all the way to church because of the overwhelming disappointment. I was convinced that my marriage was ending.

I started seeking counsel from my pastor's wife. She would meet me for coffee, breakfast or lunch on days that I felt the burden of a hurting marriage was too great to bear. I relied on friends to help walk me through such a rough patch in our marriage. My spiritual journey had managed to put a rift into our marriage. A marriage that had already endured the unthinkable. A big rift. Before I knew it, we were arguing all the time, and disagreeing on everything. I felt like I was doing all of the work, and that Wayne had checked out of this marriage.

Wayne was raised in a Catholic household. He went to a Catholic grade school. I, however, wasn't raised in any particular faith. In high school, I was told that I needed to attend Catechism, but I never took anything seriously. He was stunned when we walked through the church doors. To be honest, we both were. But still, I was hungry, spiritually hungry, for something, anything that would give me the sliver of joy that I so badly wanted again.

As I started to rely more on God, I felt my marriage separate further than ever before. I felt like the more of myself I gave to

God, the less of myself was available to Wayne. I struggled to find a balance between my two important relationships. Over time, we continued arguing and our temperaments for each other grew short.

Wayne and I would talk about our marital issues in therapy and how I was the one in this relationship that was attempting to change the rules by adding a faith element to our marriage, which we never had before. I tried everything.

I was so upset that God would bring me through something so devastating such as the death of our child, and that He would do the work to change my heart, to glorify Him, but at the same time "destroy" my marriage. It didn't make any sense to me. Things got so bad that we just entirely stopped talking to each other all together. I tried giving him two alternatives, this church or nothing. But the more I thought about it, the less I wanted to push him to go. I was ready to throw in the towel. I was prepared to surrender to the enemy. I was ready to tell him that he won and that our marriage was defeated. And perhaps the worst admittance on my part, I printed divorce papers. And the moment that I saw the papers come off the printer, my heart sank to my stomach. I began realizing what road I was about to travel down. And I didn't want to go there.

We sat down and discussed the option of legally separating. The option was never really there. But the feelings of hurt and being unloved were definitely present. I felt God tell me not to give up. So, I toughed it out. We toughed it out. The option disappeared when we realized that we both deeply loved each other and desperately wanted our family to be restored. Grief came more into perspective once we realized that a lot of this pain was actually the repercussions of the magnitude of the loss of Bo.

It wasn't until someone asked if I was praying for Wayne that things really came back into perspective for me. This wasn't a battle between me and Wayne. This wasn't a battle of Wayne not wanting fellowship with God. This was a battle of Satan not wanting to give our family up. The battles of this world are not of the flesh, there are spirits that are battling for our souls. This was a battle from the enemy and he wanted our souls back. I began praying for my husband.

I stumbled to find the words to say aloud, "God, please give my husband the strength that he needs to make it through today. Please allow his guard to come down with You and make him be the example that You made him to be. Soften Wayne's heart to the idea of going where You can be glorified the most. Please restore our marriage to its full potential and fix the brokenhearted feelings that lie in our home. Heal his heart, Lord. He is devastated by the loss of Bo, we both are. Teach us how we can confidently put our trust in You and allow us to feel peace. Jesus, I want so badly to have a godly marriage and to pray with Wayne. I want to do devotionals with him and for our marriage to have a strong foundation based on You. I know that You can do this, please make this possible. In Your name, Amen!"

I started asking others that were dedicated to fervent prayer life to pray for him. I tried looking up devotionals specifically targeting how I could become a better, more supportive and loving wife. A wife that was less abrasive and more understanding and kindhearted.

Even though it was different for Wayne, he would still agree to come to church on Sunday mornings. And, in an effort to keep the peace, I reluctantly agreed to go back to the Catholic church for one Sunday. I brought my Bible with me, just as I got used to doing at Cornerstone United Pentecostal Church. When we arrived there, we sat near the front row. I tried to look up Scripture as the priest would call it out. I felt stares and gazes for bringing my Bible into church. People looked at me like I was crazy. They started praying the Hail Mary, and I felt my eyes well up with tears. They sang hymns in the same tone, and the whole congregation followed as they stood up, kneeled and sat down together. They started saying the "Our Father" prayer that Jesus said in the Bible as an example for us to follow. I couldn't hold my feelings in. I sat in silence as I listened to the priest preach on the importance of praying in repetition. Meanwhile I couldn't shake the feeling that people were staring at us. I closed my eyes tightly and prayed. I asked God for forgiveness for being there. They finished with Communion, and I refused to partake in it.

After mass ended, we got into our van and, on the way home, Wayne apologized. He said that he felt completely uncomfortable there and I was relieved because I did too. He said, "I felt so out of place there. We need to go back to Cornerstone."

We returned home and I read scripture after scripture that I was preparing to present to Wayne. I couldn't find any scriptural references for praying to mother Mary.

Matthew 6:7 – But when ye pray, use not vain repetitions, as the heathen do: for they think that they shall be heard for their much speaking.

Matthew 23:9 – And do not call anyone on earth 'father,' for you have one Father, and he is in Heaven.

Matthew 7:15 – Beware of false prophets, which come to you in sheep's clothing, but inwardly they are ravening wolves.

I revealed all of these scriptures to Wayne and he was still in an agreement that we should go back to Cornerstone.

GOD ANSWERED MY PRAYER!

And over time, he was able to start relaying what he took out of the sermons at Cornerstone. He was present in the moment and he was so supportive the day that I decided to be baptized.

The day that I decided to give everything to Jesus was an incredibly special day in more than one way. I helped to celebrate Bo's 2nd Birthday (10/7) by being baptized in Jesus' name. I felt the rush of the Holy Spirit come upon me as I plummeted into the water. I held my nose and felt the water cover every inch of my body. My "old self" was now buried in baptism. I now had the Holy Spirit fire come to live in me.

As I arose from the water, I couldn't help but feel that the purifying waves replaced a tiny bit of the joy that was missing from my life. I looked out at my family, cried and praised God!

This was the first sliver of happiness that I felt after Bo died.

The Restoration Season

It was after this point that our marriage started, what I like to call "The Restoration Season."

Wayne and I worked extremely hard on getting to where we are now. He bent, and I bent. A lot like the Limbo. We have gone through the unimaginable together, and the work definitely needed to be done. And we knew that we weren't going to give in to the "statistics" of getting divorced after your beloved child dies. I knew that this marriage was destined by God. Even through all the struggles.

Our marriage started to slowly blossom to its full potential when we started developing a devotional life together. We would sit down after the kids went to bed and make time for us. The encouraging devotionals breathed hope into our relationship. We went from not having sex at all, to making love two times a week (sometimes more!).

We felt the restoration that God had promised. Even though it was rough beyond any measure. Even though we would argue about ridiculous things. Even though I printed out divorce papers. Our relationship was never out of God's sight. Our marriage was never out of God's plan. It just took Wayne a little bit longer to open up to God. Because God works on all of us at different times, in different ways.

I was convicted that the agony that I was living in because of Bo's death, wasn't going to be the highlight of my life. There was a greater destination. There was a greater plan in place. A divine plan.

Mourning, and being completely lost, couldn't be what I was sent here to be. It couldn't be what I was sent here to do.

I will miss Bo the rest of my life, but I wasn't intended to carry the magnitude of the loss of my child. Not on my shoulders, alone.

Paul tells us that we are able to mourn WITH hope. There are dozens of scriptures that say so, but here are some of my personal favorites:

1 Thessalonians 4:13 – Brothers and sisters, we do not want you to be uninformed about those who sleep in death, so that you do not grieve like the rest of mankind, who have no hope.

Psalm 23:4 – Even though I walk through the valley of the shadow of death, I will fear no evil, for you are with me; your rod and your staff, they comfort me.

Job 5:11 – He sets on high those who are lowly, and those who mourn are lifted to safety.

Psalm 46:1 – God is our refuge and strength, a very present help in trouble.

Matthew 5:4 – Blessed are those who mourn, for they shall be comforted.

Even if you don't believe in Jesus. Even if you don't believe that there is something after this life. You've been prayed for. By yours truly. Because we are called to intercede for others if and when they're hurting. Interceding with prayer. I'm so thankful that God removed the scales from my eyes.

So, when you have a friend that is going through heartache, you have an obligation to intercede with prayer for them.

They might be mad at God. They might not understand why they are walking through the valley that they are. They might not understand or like the season that they are currently in. And it is by the power of your prayer that you could help.

Does that mean that it's all "cakes and pies?" Because I gave my life to God, will I struggle anymore? The answer is YES! We are actually PROMISED heartache. We're guaranteed agony. Turmoil. Devastation. Heartbreak. This doesn't make me any better than you. Or you better than me. Because we both fall short of the glory of God. Every single time.

But what Jesus gives me, is the ability to give it to Him. Instead of holding onto things that were designed to be left at His feet. And He can do that for you too!

Just because I decided to dedicate my life to God doesn't mean everything gets better. In fact, it's quite the contrary. The devil will work harder to win your soul back. Don't give it to him. It doesn't always get easier.

I have, and continue to, suffer from chronic anxiety and depression. I could still be totally happy one minute, and the next feel completely overwhelmed with emotion. I do my very best to deal with the feelings as they come. But the best thing that I have learned, is to be honest with my family and friends.

To be completely honest and communicate everything that I'm feeling, I first had to start with my husband. Since Wayne was around me the majority of the time, and he knew me practically better than I knew myself, I thought that this was the most appropriate avenue to start with. Before I realized it made more sense to be honest and communicate, I would get so upset with Wayne because he couldn't read my mind. The majority of our fights started because I would be upset and then get more upset because Wayne wouldn't pick up the little hints that I would drop about being bothered or mad.

A simple heads-up to my husband:

"Wayne, I'm feeling off today."

"Babe, I'm just feeling depressed."

"I'm feeling anxious."

Whatever I would be feeling in that moment, I would muster up the courage to tell my husband. Even though I sometimes feel like a failure. Even though I feel guilty for feeling depressed even though I have Jesus. But I go out on a limb and let my husband in. Do you know what he does?

He comforts me. He still to this day, comforts me. I have probably come to him hundreds of times. And each time, he never lets me down. And this carries over into every other friendship and relationship I have in my life. The importance of being completely honest and letting people know when my anxiety is flaring up has rendered many relationships.

As we grow spiritually together, I'm still a work in progress. We both are. Just like you. I'm no different. We're all human.

Human. The human mind.

What a beautiful, yet sophisticated torture chamber. From the very moment we enter this world, we are biologically programmed to fix things. When trauma happens, your mind becomes its own private circus. The only difference is that you have a free admission into the circus every single time. Sometimes its involuntary, the thoughts and feelings. And sometimes you welcome it.

This is why you need people to rely on. The importance of surrounding yourself with people who uplift you, and love you is impeccable.

But when it starts to get dark, I turn to:

Jeremiah 29:11 – "For I know the plans I have for you," declares the Lord, "plans to prosper you and not to harm you, plans to give you hope and a future."

A whirlwind of blissful memories that are trampled by the aggressiveness that bleeds from the hurricane that we call grief. It is so important to read things that uplift you.

The beautiful thing is that when we realize that we're not alone, confidence starts to breed. The confidence that we can depend on others. Once we find out that other parents have LIVED through this debilitating loss, we immediately feel a connection to them. The ones that have the child loss veil. The ones that have lost their innocence.

Child loss is something that can be so alienating. It can often make you feel so lonely. There is power in numbers and it truly takes a village to get through this. You're not alone.

But HE can do WAY more than I, or any other parent of child loss, ever could!

Jeremiah 29:13 – You will seek me and find me when you seek me with all your heart.

God will see us through. He always does. And the biggest task is getting through the anger that is harbored. That I think every parent who faces the death of their child goes through.

And because I put my faith in Jesus Christ, I know that I will see my son again, and with that, I have a responsibility to help get my husband to this point, I have a responsibility to help my kids get to this point, I have a responsibility to help get YOU to this point.

Together, we can do this. We can walk through the trenches of child loss together. We are battered and bruised, together. We are warriors, together. We can walk through loss, together.

You are not alone.

The craziest part out of all of this is that if I didn't have the chance to be entrusted with such a magnificent little boy, and if I didn't feel the worst pain of my life, I would have never been saved. I wasn't truly saved before because I didn't dedicate my life to Christ. I was a *holiday* Christian. And the truth is, I wasn't cutting it with God. He didn't want just weekend worship; God wanted a relationship with me. He desires one with all of us. I would be absolutely lost without Him by my side. I'm so thankful that God has trusted me, someone that was a nobody, with people's lives at their most vulnerable moments.

And please understand that Bo is NOT an angel. God has His angels. God made His angels. They were with Him at the beginning of creation. Bo is a child of God. Thank You Jesus for that! I have confidence that Bo is up there with Jesus, and they are having the best time ever. I also believe that for every loss family that we meet down here, our children have met in Heaven. It brings me so much comfort to picture this.

If you or someone you know is struggling with the death of their child, don't wait. Every second is crucial. It's a matter of life and death for the parents. They need hope fast. I know because I was one of them. I walked through the darkest valley. And I'm here to report back and tell you that you can do this.

And sweet mama, and daddy, you did NOT lose your child. You never LOST them. You know exactly where they are. Heaven. With the King of Kings, and all of our other children that have gone before us.

We can do this together. We can transform perspective. We can breathe hope into each other's lives. We can encourage and be there for each other on our worst days. Its biblical. We were created for community. We were created for fellowship. There is a family out there that will love you to the fullest capacity. God will mend every crack in your heart. If you come home to Him.

My hope is that this book will be somewhat of a survival guide. Whether you've experienced the death of your child or not, you need saving. Because there is a very real enemy that is on the hunt for your soul. And if you have experienced the death of your child, or someone in your family has, I'm here to tell you that the reward isn't worth the risk. Seek salvation. Talk to God. And He will restore you. It's in His Word. It's in His Promise to us. He desires to be with us. He desires to have a relationship. But God's a gentleman, he isn't going to knock your door down. The Bible says that God will stand at the door and knock:

Revelation 3:20 – Here I am! I stand at the door and knock. If anyone hears my voice and opens the door, I will come in and eat with that person, and they with me.

He will deliver you, redeem you, and make you whole again. With God's hand you will soar on wings like eagles. You'll find rest that you never knew was possible. The emptiness that you're feeling, that's the absence of joy, and joy only comes from the Lord. With Jesus, you can find your joy again! If you can just trust Him. God never left me in my valley because He is faithful. The days that I felt so alone and cried out to Him, He heard it. The valleys are where we grow the most, spiritually. And He is there, every step of the way.

The pain of your child dying never goes away, you just learn to wear it better. Like a small pebble that was once a boulder, and that slowly transformed over time to be something a little more manageable to carry, in your pocket. Grief never leaves you. It just changes.

So, decide. Decide whether you want to live the rest of your life in this agony and hopelessness that the devil promises. It's all about perception. If you want to believe that your child is in a better place, Heaven, or if they really are "lost." Decide whether you want to take a leap of faith, and trust God. Fully trust Him. I know it hurts. And sometimes you feel that you cannot go on. I've been there. I still go there. I try very hard to remember how important it is to read His Word, pray bold prayers, ask other people to pray for me and with me. Renew your strength by giving God these worries, anxieties and struggles. Through Him, everything, anything, all things are possible.

We turned our tragedy into triumph, and you can too. You can do this! The most important thing to remember is to be gentle and patient with yourself because you are your worst critic. God is waiting patiently for you to decide. He's not as hard on you as you are on yourself.

I'm praying for you. Fervently, praying for you.

And in the end, we will sing and dance with praise. We will rejoice because we will be with them again, and we will all be home. In Heaven.

2 Corinthians 1:3-5 – Praise be to the God and Father of our Lord Jesus Christ, the Father of compassion and the God of all comfort, who comforts us in all our troubles, so that we can comfort those in any trouble with the comfort we ourselves receive from God. For just as we share abundantly in the sufferings of Christ, so also our comfort abounds through Christ. If we are distressed, it is for your comfort and salvation; if we are comforted, it is for your comfort, which produces in you patient endurance of the same sufferings we suffer. And our hope for you is firm, because we know that just as you share in our sufferings, so also you share in our comfort.

All Biblical pieces (unless otherwise noted) have been used in reference to: The YouVersion Bible Application, New International Version (NIV).

To get involved with donations, volunteering, or to take action now visit:

www.bosheavenlyclubhouse.com
www.facebook.com/bosheavenlyclubhouse
or call 262.388.4290

We are ALWAYS open.

Follow Bo's Heavenly Clubhouse on Social Media!
Instagram: @bosheavenlyclubhouse
Twitter: @BoClubhouse

9 781645 381181